S⁻

The
Good
Life

The Christian Practice of Everyday Life

David S. Cunningham
and William T. Cavanaugh, series editors

This series seeks to present specifically Christian perspectives on some of the most prevalent contemporary practices of everyday life. It is intended for a broad audience—including clergy, interested laypeople, and students. The books in this series are motivated by the conviction that, in the contemporary context, Christians must actively demonstrate that their allegiance to the God of Jesus Christ always takes priority over secular structures that compete for our loyalty—including the state, the market, race, class, gender, and other functional idolatries. The books in this series will examine these competing allegiances as they play themselves out in particular day-to-day practices, and will provide concrete descriptions of how the Christian faith might play a more formative role in our everyday lives.

The Christian Practice of Everyday Life series is an initiative of The Ekklesia Project, an ecumenical gathering of pastors, theologians, and lay leaders committed to helping the church recall its status as the distinctive, real-world community dedicated to the priorities and practices of Jesus Christ and to the inbreaking Kingdom of God. (For more information on The Ekklesia Project, see <www.ekklesiaproject.org>.)

The Good Life

GENUINE CHRISTIANITY

for the MIDDLE CLASS

THE CHRISTIAN PRACTICE OF EVERYDAY LIFE Series

David Matzko McCarthy

Brazos Press

A Division of Baker Book House Co
Grand Rapids, Michigan 49516

Published by Brazos Press
a division of Baker Book House Company
P.O. Box 6287, Grand Rapids, MI 49516–6287
www.brazospress.com

Printed in the United States of America

Library of Congress Cataloging-in-Publication Data is on file at the Library of Congress,
Washington, D.C.

ISBN 1-58743-068-1

To Bridget

*Thank you for the ordinary days
that have made our first ten years
wonderful.*

Contents

Contents

Acknowledgments

■ This book was put to paper during an eventful year, and the labor as well as the satisfaction of the work can be measured in hours of missed sleep. In this sense, studying and writing are somewhat like pregnancy and childbirth. I say "somewhat like childbirth" because I certainly do not want to elevate a book to the significance of bearing and nurturing children. However, during our son Daniel's first year of life, I was writing this book, and it is hard to avoid an analogy between the two. In each case, a lot of sleep was missed, yet the experience of each was so energizing that missed sleep mattered little. Indeed, it is true that many people do not sleep when delighted as well as agitated, and with children it is sometimes hard to separate one form of sleeplessness from the other. So, it is with writing a book. The struggles and joys are woven together.

Writing this book, like witnessing the beginning of Daniel's life, has given me a clear sense of what I owe to others and, of course, to our God. I thank the theology faculty at Mount Saint Mary's College for their help, and my freshman seminar and moral theology classes for talking through the issues with me. I thank Charlotte Horning for editing the entire manuscript and, at key moments, pressing significant changes upon me. Because of the research and writing of the book, life in our house has been scrutinized and changed. I thank Bridget, my wife, for her seriousness, adventuresome spirit and her hospitality. I should also express gratitude to our children, Abigail, Quin, Jack, and Daniel, who never say no to prayers or to mud puddles. The combination is both wonderful and exasperating. Like them, I suspect that this book will annoy the reader at a few points and amuse at others. In the process, I hope that it will refine our trust in following Jesus' way and our hope in God's mercy and grace. It is written to Christians who desire to live more faithfully.

The Beginning:
Seek First the Kingdom

■ When my brother and his wife were married, they chose Matthew 6:25–34 as the Gospel reading. This portion of Jesus' Sermon on the Mount begins with, "Do not worry about your life, what you will eat or what you will drink." Jesus counsels us to look at the birds of the air and the lilies of the field. "If God so clothes the grass of the field, which is alive today and tomorrow is thrown into the oven, will he not much more clothe you—you of little faith?" (v. 30). We are told not to worry about what we will eat, drink, and wear, but to "strive first for the kingdom of God and his righteousness, and all these things will be given to you as well" (v. 33). It has been twenty years since I heard these verses read at my brother's wedding. I remember being impressed. I must have been impressed, because I can hardly remember the Gospel text from my own wedding only ten years ago.

I was just about twenty-one years old at my brother's wedding, and the reading of Matthew 6 reached my ears with a sense of excitement. I was intrigued. "Could marriage and family life be lived with this spirit of the gospel?" The text seemed to fit the occasion perfectly. My brother was enrolled in Candler School of Theology at the time, and his wife had just graduated from college. They were just about to embark on their own adventure. They were married in her home church, which was a handsome and unpretentious Methodist church in rural Connecticut. Their friends and family played prominent roles in the ceremony and in taking charge of the weekend events. For example, the home congregation prepared the reception and meals. Their wedding became my guiding image of faithful living, and Matthew 6 was a charter for the happy home.

Ten years later my wife and I were married, and by that time my attitude toward "the birds of the air" and "the lilies of the field" had changed. I was thirty, and my pragmatic side was leading the way. I had lost sight of the idealistic side of the counsel, "Strive first for the kingdom of God." Matthew 6:25–34 concludes with, "So do not worry about tomorrow, for tomorrow will bring worries of its own. Today's trouble is enough for today." I was worrying plenty about tomorrow. But today, after ten years of marriage and four children, a strange thing is starting to happen. The troubles and demands of daily life (of work, home, and neighborhood) are starting to be all that I can handle. In fact, *we* handle it; I really do not handle anything alone. The strange thing is that I am starting to understand striving for the kingdom of God anew. I am starting to see that "seek first the kingdom of God" is not idealistic advice, but a very practical way of love.

This practical way of God's love is the topic of this book. Listen to the practical possibilities in the verse (emphasis mine), "Strive first for the kingdom of God and his righteousness, *and all these things will be given to you as well.*" A few years ago (perhaps longer than that), I set out to understand the implications of this advice. Now, I am just starting to feel the impact of this search. Researching and writing a book changes a person's life. An author lives so near and so long with a set of problems and ideas that they become companions, and my companions have been the Gospels, particularly the Gospels of Matthew and Luke, as well as the church's tradition of reflection on the love of God, people, and creation. I have listened to fourth-century preachers like John Chrysostom and desert ascetics like Antony and Synclitica of Egypt. They have challenged me to change my life. I hope that you hear their realistic and practical challenge in my words. Together, we will hear the call to be saints.

The Book in Outline

This book is divided into four parts: people, places, things, and God and creation. Each part offers a contrast between our regular and routine ways of living and a renewal of our lives through God's grace.

As the subtitle of this book suggests, we will be considering middle-class life in the United States. We will be concerned particularly with the power of our market economy to shape and govern our everyday relationships to people, places, and things. In our time, the market is an invasive force. Our growth economy is impressive in its capacity to make products available to the consumer, but it is also daunting in its ability to become part of nearly all aspects of our lives.

The economy forms a landscape where we are invited to live happily. The benefits of our standard of living cannot be denied. Nevertheless, I will propose that we think about the kingdom of God as a contrasting horizon. In contrast to the "dwelling place" of the market, this book will inquire about our relationships and purposes in the household of God. Consider this book an exercise in thinking about the difference made by God's unmerited love for the world.

The "household" is an image which is woven through this entire book. The idea of a household suggests kinship, as we are all children of God, and it also includes questions of income and resources, cooperation, mutual care, and common goals. We have important theological questions to ask: How are our relationships to people, places, and things properly understood if God is our creator and our common destiny? How do we properly use things if this is God's world? What happens to our dwelling places when we are open to the hospitality of God?

In reference to the household, the story of Zacchaeus (Luke 19:1–10) provides a key theme. You may recall that Zacchaeus is a tax collector who climbs a tree in order to see Jesus from above a crowd. Zacchaeus just wants a look, but to his surprise, Jesus addresses him directly and invites himself to Zacchaeus's home. Jesus' entry into Zacchaeus's household is a strange kind of hospitality. We are not accustomed to people inviting themselves to our dinner table. Indeed, God's hospitality is strange to human ways. By inviting himself in, God draws near to us with the fullness of grace.

The story of Zacchaeus ends with the transformation of his home, his way of doing business, and his relationships to his neighbors (that is, to his fellow Jews). Jesus declares that Zacchaeus, once set against God and his neighbor, has been restored and salvation has come upon his home. Throughout this book, the story of Zacchaeus is used as a parable for receiving grace amid our homes, our way of doing business, and our relationships with our neighbors.

Part 1 emphasizes themes of God's hospitality and friendship.

- Christians profess faith that God befriends the world through the self-giving love of Jesus Christ. Part 1 seeks to understand our everyday lives in the light of God's self-revelation and friendship.
- With the light of Christ, we can gain a new perspective on our relationships and our role in the world. For example, in American culture, friendship, love, and faith are usually cordoned off within a private sphere of personal pleasures and preferences. In such a context, the friendship of God is disruptive. God's hospitality draws

us outside of ourselves, and outside the safety of our private homes and planned neighborhoods. As Christians, we are called to gather in God's name, to be open to God's grace, and to make a difference by being transformed by God's friendship.

- An important example for this part of the book is the story of the rich young man (Matt. 19:16–22). In Matthew 19:20, we are told that the young man has done his best to follow the commands of God. He asks Jesus if there is anything else that he needs to do in order to attain eternal life. "What do I still lack?" Jesus tells him that he lacks nothing, but that he has too much. The young man is instructed to give away his possessions and to follow Jesus. Hearing this command, he departs in sadness for he cannot free himself from his belongings.

- Watching the interchange between their teacher and the young man, the disciples ask Jesus who can be saved if not the rich. If the rich are not blessed, then who is? Who can be saved if not the blessed and the righteous? Jesus replies, "For mortals it is impossible, but for God all things are possible" (Matt. 19:26). The account of the rich young man's question to Jesus provides a parable of grace.

- This parable of grace suggests a contradiction in our usual way of thinking about riches and poverty. For us, the contradiction is that an abundance of things may very well make us poor. In our pursuit of things, we may become too deeply focused on security and individual freedom to enjoy the adventure of God's love. We may be so attached to having things that we become detached from the world. The challenge of grace is to see and respond to the bounty of God's friendship—the bounty of community with God and our neighbors.

Part 2 deals with the idea of place in two ways—first in terms of cultivating a dwelling place of hospitality and friendship, and second in terms of our role as Christians in the world.

- Part 2 begins with a theme that was introduced in Part 1, the theme of Jesus' homelessness. The theme is represented by Matthew 8:20, "Foxes have holes, and birds of the air have nests; but the Son of Man has nowhere to lay his head." In Part 1, I propose that Jesus' homelessness is hardly a flight from the world. On the contrary, his homelessness means that the Son of God has drawn near, that he makes his home with us—that "though he was in the form of God, did not regard equality with God as something to be exploited, but emptied himself, taking the form of a slave, being born in human likeness" (Phil. 2:6–7).

- Through the incarnation of God in Christ, the Son of God is sent to join with human life. In following the one who is sent to us, we are called to make our home in the world, but to do so in the peace and hospitality of Christ. Recall, once again, the story of Zacchaeus. As we entertain Jesus in our homes, we receive grace, and our lives are transformed.

- We usually think about modern society as being very "worldly"—as enjoying and being satisfied with the fullness of earthly existence. I suggest the contrary. In the modern world there is a strong desire for flight from ordinary life. There is a desire to be free and to detach ourselves from the people and things that bind us in the world. In Part 2, I characterize this desire for detachment as a flight to "no place." In contrast, Christians are called to cultivate a particular place and to be open (as Zacchaeus is) to the hospitality of God.

- Part 2 concludes with a contrast between violence and hope. When we are deeply bound to our purposes in the world, depending upon violence is an ever-present temptation. Violence is efficient and effective for removing obstacles to our goals. Usually, people and nations turn to violence in order to do some good—to do what they firmly believe is right and good. In other words, violence is a popular means to take control and get things done. In contrast, we Christians are called to live by (to live out and to live for) God's reconciliation and peace. To depend upon God's grace requires that we take on risks (and court failure in the process). In faith, we take on what we cannot do alone. In other words, to live faithfully requires that we live with hope.

- Christian hope is not a vague optimism or cheerfulness. It is faith that God's purposes will be fulfilled, that the love of God in Jesus Christ will not be defeated by the powers of hatred, violence, and injustice in the world. Hope is the activity of faith in Jesus. It is by faith, hope, and God's love that Christians take their place in the world.

The main points of Part 3 are that our relation to things ought to cultivate common life with our neighbors, and that our proper relation to the earth depends upon our relationship to God.

- Part 3 begins with the suggestion that our usual way of ascribing economic value gives very little meaning to things. Market value does not correspond to the significance and function of things in our lives.

- One reason for this lack of correspondence between price and value is that a healthy market economy encourages us to dispense with the old and acquire the new. The market cannot sustain us because the significance of things requires a shared history and identity. In contrast to the new and improved, that which endures makes its way deeply into our lives. In light of this contrast, I make what might seem to be a strange claim: the market economy fosters an "otherworldly" attitude. Consumer capitalism is marked by a flight from the world, particularly into the sphere of private pleasures.

- In Part 3, I propose that consumerism is motivated by a desire for otherworldly happiness. In consumer culture, "otherworldly happiness" is sought through feelings or pleasures that allow us to transcend the routines and experiences of our ordinary lives. The consumer economy promises great benefits, but ironically, it makes our everyday lives nearly impossible to manage. Evidence for this claim can be seen in the recent escalation of consumer debt and personal bankruptcies. Amid the excesses of the market, the acquisition of things is not giving us the happiness that we desire. Instead, we are likely to become possessed by our possessions. We become indebted to things.

- "Seek first the kingdom of God" is the antidote to our slavery to things and a corresponding sense of meaninglessness. Through an entirely different kind of economy, God's reign is founded on the gift of the Son, and we are freed by that gift. Faith in the grace of God is the beginning of freedom and the possibility of deep attachments in the world. When our relationship to God is set in order, we are able to see and enjoy the fullness of things.

Part 4, titled "God and Creation," brings the themes of the first three parts together through a treatment of the Nicene Creed. The principle theme of Part 4 is the almost unimaginable grace of God, which makes possible our fulfillment in the love of people, places, and things.

- This last part of the book marks a shift in emphasis. The first three parts focused on our relationships and our habits of everyday life. The "household" was the representative image, and the story of Zacchaeus served as a parable of God's hospitality in our homes. Part 4, in comparison, gives specific attention to our words rather than our actions (but includes our actions as well). Put better, this part of the book looks at discipleship from the viewpoint of the

Christian confession of faith. Our profession of faith (in the Nicene Creed) forms the structure and content of this part.

- I begin this part by dividing the first line of the creed in two: "We believe in One God, the Father, the Almighty, maker of heaven and earth." For the purposes of the book, I discuss "we believe" in relation to how we remember and *think through* our baptism—how we understand our lives from our beginning in the grace of God. From this point I turn to the love of God for creation. The grace of Jesus Christ is the point from which we Christians proclaim that God is "the maker of heaven and earth." Jesus Christ is the gift through which we know that creation is a gift from God, who is love.

- The second article of the creed, "We believe in One Lord, Jesus Christ, the only Son of God," provides occasion for me to reintroduce the theme of Jesus' homelessness: the Son empties himself in order to take his place among us, for our salvation (Phil. 2:6–11). Developing this theme, I use the genealogy in Matthew 1:1–17 in order to underline the unique character of Jesus' kingship. He is the king who is raised up among the lowly. The reign of God is inaugurated from within the twists and turns, successes and failures, faithfulness and sin of human inheritance. From within this history, Jesus offers a way of reconciliation and peace, which we are called to follow in his Spirit.

- "We believe in the Holy Spirit, the Lord, the giver of life." In reference to this article of the creed, I discuss the preaching of John the Baptist (Luke 3:1–20) and the sending out of the disciples in Matthew 10:5–15. Each passage provides a way to consider discipleship in terms of Jesus' homelessness and his call for us to "seek first the kingdom of God" (Matt. 6:33). Each passage gives us a way of seeing God's hospitality. In Matthew 10:5–15, the disciples are sent into the countryside, into villages and towns. They are instructed to proclaim that "the kingdom of heaven has come near" (Matt. 10:7). It is interesting in this regard that they are told, as well, to accept and depend upon the hospitality of the people and towns. They are like Jesus who brings new life to Zacchaeus by entering into his home.

- Along with our profession of faith "in the Holy Spirit," we affirm that "we believe in the one holy catholic and apostolic church" and that "we acknowledge one baptism for the forgiveness of sins." These statements of the creed provide occasion for me to emphasize and develop the book's proposals about the Christian's place and role in the world. The church is constituted by ordinary people who are gathered to live an alternative way. This new way is founded on everyday practices of worship and common life. The grace and

17

practices of forgiveness are central to our way of community with God and neighbor.

- Part 4 concludes with a discussion of the final line of the creed, "We look for the resurrection of the dead, and the life of the world to come." Here, I underline a key claim of the book: the body and spirit cannot be divided, and the way of the Spirit cannot be separated from our place among people and our use of things. I begin this chapter with Paul's assurances about the resurrection of the body in 1 Corinthians 15:12–58. I conclude by telling about the life of Antony, a third-century Christian who sought after "poverty of spirit" in the Egyptian desert. Antony desired to be guided by the Holy Spirit and to live a life of prayer and dependence upon God. His advice to fellow Christians sums up the point of this entire book. "Do not trust your own righteousness, do not worry about the past, but control your tongue and your stomach." Indeed, in this book, I have attempted to transplant Antony's desert wisdom to the jungle of middle-class life.

Part 1

People

Introduction

■ The first part of this book focuses on the love of people. Although the aim of this book is to better understand God's love, the love of those who stand with us and near us is usually the most obvious and the most pressing kind of love. By beginning with the love of people, I will be able to emphasize the joys and burdens of love and our desires for happiness and rest. This first part begins with the burdens of wealth and the sorrow of the rich young man. In Matthew's Gospel, the good and conscientious young man, a follower of God's law, walks away sadly after Jesus tells him to sell his possessions and to give his wealth to the poor (Matt. 19:16–22). In contrast to this call to give everything away, I juxtapose the disruptiveness of God's friendship, not as austerity imposed upon the world, but as unimaginable plenty. Here is the irony. John the Baptist comes out of the desert announcing the coming of our Lord. He is dressed in camel's hair, and he subsists upon locusts and wild honey. But the Lord who comes brings bounty; he gives us a seat at a wedding banquet. "For John came neither eating nor drinking, and they say, 'He has a demon'; the Son of Man came eating and drinking, and they say, 'Look, a glutton and a drunkard, a friend of tax collectors and sinners!'" (Matt. 11:18–19).

God's friendship is our riches. "Come to me, all you that are weary and are carrying heavy burdens, and I will give you rest. . . . For my yoke is easy, and my burden is light" (Matt. 11:28–30).

1

American and Middle Class

■ When our daughter was in first grade, she asked her mother and me if we were rich. We were surprised by her question, and after a short conversation we discovered that her question originated from two sources. The first was her experiences at school, where she had encountered children from more affluent families than those in our neighborhood. She had spent a few afternoons playing in a schoolmate's home, in a house that was far larger, far newer, and far better furnished than ours. The contrast in homes, I suppose, was clear even to a six-year-old child. (Or, perhaps her friend's abundant Barbie collection was the clue.) The second source of her question was her innocent hearing of various readings from the Gospels and our prayers for the poor. We seemed to be praying for the poor, but we did not seem wealthy. Abigail asked if we were rich because she wanted to know where we stood in the scheme of things.

"We are rich," that was our answer. We told Abigail that some kids at school and people in our area have more money and better things than we do, but in relation to most people in the world we are very rich. We have more than we need, but most of all we have plenty to eat, a secure house, and warm beds. Then I continued on until long after she was listening. I even brought the topic up this year when Abigail was preparing a report on colonial times. We discovered that children worked most of the day, and when they did play, they used homemade toys—toys they had made for themselves. I had to dwell for a while on that bit of information.

22

Poor Abigail, she is the oldest child of a teacher, and she must hear the rough draft of every parental lecture. She is also the granddaughter of a woman who was raised during the Great Depression and later spent several years raising her own children as a single mother on her income as a waitress. Long after, when my mother could afford to live comfortably, she still smoothed out and washed, used, and reused her aluminum foil. She kept the thermostat at 62° in the winter. She took pride in her yard-sale bargains, and she liked to haggle and barter. She'd probably cut your hair if you'd mow her lawn. We have in our home now (since her death) several of her treasured items, such as quilts, a daybed, and a desk. Our family's favorite is her thirty-year-old recliner that has been reupholstered three or four times. It is now plain blue, a clear image of my mother's simple approach to things.

"We are rich." It was a bit of a confession for me. I was raised with a definite sense that other families had more than we did. Being raised with little, moving upward but still "not rich" has become part of my identity, and I suspect that I share this identity with many middle-class Americans. We are a people who like to look forward, to expand and improve, so that we are not inclined to dwell on the fact that we have more than others. Many of us who are heirs of English colonists and European immigrants have grown together in this upward direction. The same holds for middle-class Americans whose forebears were slaves and sharecroppers, or whose parents and grandparents were migrant farm workers. Many of us are descendents of farmers and laborers, who through the generations of the twentieth century have advanced along with others in our country. In our neighborhoods and towns it is sometimes hard to notice that we have become rich. We know our day-to-day struggles and pains, our failures and drawbacks, and our hard work, worry, and anxiety about money. Many of us live in a rich land without feeling affluent.

The day after Abigail asked if we were rich, I told some students about our conversation. College students are very kind and patient with me when I go on about my children. I cannot help using their innocent questions as the basis for serious discussions. On this occasion, I was surprised when several students showed discomfort with my declaration of being rich. One young woman replied with an awkward, "Good for you." She was worried that I might be including her among the privileged class. She, like her classmates, faces an economic world of uncertainties. In fact, the expense of her college education is a venture on job security. She knows the financial burdens carried by her parents. Like many, she will incur debt in order to receive her degree, her professional training, and her certification (this student intends to become a registered nurse). She is entertained by rich people everyday, whether actors, musicians,

23

or professional athletes. They are making millions or billions; she (like me) is just plodding along.

I imagine that a good number of the millionaires and billionaires think of themselves in the same way: just trudging along with their burdens and worries, seeing their riches around them (which are also their worries) but not thinking about themselves as rich. Every extravagance in their lives provides a well-deserved diversion or opportunity for relaxation and rest. Like these imagined millionaires, I do not think of myself as rich. When I look at what is immediately before me, I see my hard work and many people who have more than I do. However, when I look just a little bit further across the border or tracks, I see a different world. I see that I have, at least comparatively, great prosperity and day-to-day freedom from the wind, the cold, and threats to my well-being.

This insight puts Jesus' well known encounter with the rich young man in a different light (Matt. 19:16–22). The man asks Jesus what he must do to inherit eternal life. He notes that he has followed all the commands, but he still wonders if there is anything that he lacks. Jesus' answer is surprising: he lacks nothing, but he has too much. Jesus tells the young man to give what he has away. "If you wish to be perfect, go, sell your possessions, and give the money to the poor, and you will have treasure in heaven; then come, follow me" (Matt. 19:21). The young man goes away grieving ("for he had many possessions"), and Jesus explains to his disciples that "it will be hard for a rich person to enter the kingdom of heaven" (v. 23). They are shocked. "Then who can be saved?" Jesus' response is that salvation is impossible for us but possible for God. All is grace.

There is an additional message for me (if not for the original rich young man). The man goes away grieving for what he has lost (in his desire to keep what he has). I would not have gone away grieving, but shocked, dumbfounded. Am I rich? All I seem to have are bills and expenses, work, home repairs, money worries, and income taxes. Give my money away? Isn't everyone already taking it? By recognizing myself as rich, I am forced to rethink who I am. For the poor, burdens are imposed. The poor must trudge on with what they have. But for the rich, burdens are acquired and maintained through the never-ending work of achievement and security. Like the rich, have I *acquired* what I lack? Do my habits of working, maintaining a home, and going about the tasks of everyday life direct me away from the kingdom of heaven? Like the rich young man, does what I possess keep me from being who I ought to be?

This question of who a person ought to be is an ancient one. Greek philosophers thought that the answer was directly related to what we set about to attain, whether glory and honor in battle, wealth, fame, or the good standing of a noble citizen. What is the goal and end of life? These questions are not simply individual choices but ways and habits of living with others and pursing common goods and purposes in life. Goals and purposes in life direct us to the usefulness of one thing or another. The purposes of home determine the type and function of our furnishings, and the goals of work determine "the tools of the trade." The goals and purposes of life direct us to the usefulness of talents and virtues that are needed to make our way along the journey, to whom we befriend and who will guide us. In this first chapter on people, I am attempting to honestly introduce the question of who I ought to be from where I am in the world: American and middle class.

The United States of America is an imperial power. It might not seem so to us in America, from our neighborhoods and playgrounds and in light of our long hours of work and the bills that pile up in the mailbox. Nonetheless, we are members of the richest and most powerful country in the world today. Certainly riches and sophisticated weapons do not necessarily make a country an imperial power. On the contrary, the U.S. builds coalitions, gives aid to developing countries, sells weapons (sometimes almost gives them away), and trains soldiers of other military powers. Our government does not, like the empires of old, seek to expand through colonizing territories and imposing its own military rule and the law of its emperor or queen. However, we in the U.S. carry the weight of a rich and powerful nation.

Half a century after World War II and well over a decade after the Cold War, the U.S. economy has expanded all over the world. Our military strength and economic leverage are required to protect markets and to sustain our access to resources such as oil and cheap labor. Stability in the oil-rich lands of the Middle East has a direct relationship to economic health at home. Stability in Asia and Latin America has a direct relationship to what I am able to afford at my local store. This is not the imperialism of former empires like Britain, Spain, and Rome, but like the old empires, our economic empire gains its life and power from continuous growth. This need for growth means that our own economy must find ever-new and interesting ways to increase its role in our lives.

Our imperial economy either expands at a considerable rate or dies. Our economy survives by finding new markets, new ways to consume, new needs, and new products to advance. In the days after the terrorist attacks of September 11, 2001, Americans began to mourn and to worry about the effects of terror—of living with anxiety and fear. What can we do? Our leaders told us to go about our business, to go to work, to travel by air, to continue to vacation (especially in New York), and to go out as before—to play at the park, to drive the highways, and to shop.

To stop, to stay in our homes, and to obey a strange kind of imposed Sabbath, these are some of the worrisome effects of terrorism on the country as a whole. During World War II, countries on both sides imposed austerity and thrift upon their citizens. Many were asked to die. During the war on terror, we are asked to continue on as before, to expand and to spend. We are waging a battle of confidence in growth. We are asked to use and desire more. We in the U.S. know that the terrorists would have claimed an even greater victory if the country had stopped for a week or month to mourn. The danger in grieving is that we might rest and, in doing so, fall behind. To stop in order to mourn would have been to admit a measure of defeat. An imperial economy shows its power in its tirelessness and in its irresistible promise of freedom to grow, to have and do more.

We should stop for a moment and ask if we have allowed our economy to encroach upon aspects of our lives that ought to be free from it. Are we too easily following the promises of a strong economy? We are promised and usually given choices, convenience, pleasures, good health, and low prices. But is it possible that we are hardly free? For instance, compared to other parts of the world, we Americans pay little for a gallon of gasoline, and evidence of this fact can be seen in our standard of living and the size and number of our cars. Perhaps we should stop and ask what options are closed to us when we are unable to do without our automobiles. Must we always be on the move?

In Genesis 1:1–2:3, God's seven days of creation include and culminate in the day of rest. The Sabbath speaks of the peace that is both the beginning and the end of creation. God's peaceful and gracious "attachment" to creation is very different from the way that we human beings are attached to the people, places, and things of the earth. This difference in attachment and love is a central theme of this book, which will be developed more directly in Part 4. For now, let it suffice to point out that God's creation is a gift that adds nothing to God, and likewise, God's continuous creative activity is the full outward flowing of self-giving love. This love is revealed to us through the incarnation of God in Jesus Christ, who comes to us, lives, and dies in an outward flowing offer of love. "Foxes have holes, and birds of the air have nests; but the Son of Man has nowhere to lay his head" (Matt. 8:20). Yes, Jesus has "nowhere to lay his head," but his homelessness among us is a consequence of his "self-emptying" and "attachment" to where we make our homes. In taking on human flesh, the Son takes up our home in creation and shows the way to God.

Utterly unlike our self-giving God, we are fulfilled through taking our place in creation. People, places, and things become part of who we are—by necessity and in the particulars of our everyday lives—for the good of our fulfillment as human beings. We find our way, then, not by an escape from things, but by imitating the self-giving attachment of God,

26

in our distinctively human way, through the abundant grace of the way given to us in Jesus Christ.

The rich young man is asked to sell all he has and to follow Jesus. However, Jesus' call for dispossession is hardly a lesson in detachment from the world. On the contrary, if the rich young man is asked to follow, then he is being sent out into the world. He is being called to discipleship, and like the disciples, he will he sent out into the countryside, cities, and towns (Matt. 10:5–15). The rich young man is asked to risk a greater bond, to walk with others, to put on the clothes of discipleship and to carry the tools of peace, to depend upon the hospitality and grace of his hosts, to remain with others as their guests and to call their homes his own. The disciple's journey is one of stopping and staying, resting and eating, and bringing peace.

This book will compare two kinds of intinerancy. One is following Jesus, and the other is the restlessness of the market economy. While discipleship binds us, the market brings detachment. Certainly our modern economy encourages a strong attachment to possessions and activities of acquisition. For example, we become attached to long hours of work and its benefits. Between 1989 and 1998, middle-class family income has increased along with the hours spent at work (on average there has been an increase of four and a half full-time weeks per year for each family). Recently, there is even a strong attachment to the family. There is, however, an ease of detachment. We Americans are on the move. In reference to family, I really do not need to mention the relative ease of divorce. Undoubtedly a divorce causes sorrow and pain, but we manage to split up and move on. Even without a high rate of divorce, detachment is part of family. We marry and start "new" families, and then we are off. We move far from the "old" family in order to pursue education and work. We follow the job, and jobs follow the economy.

Even in our own homes and neighborhoods, our lives are divided and detached. Many of us live far from where we earn our wages and do business. The suburbs help set us apart from work and from various risks and insecurities of other "less desirable" neighborhoods. The relationships that might bind us deeply, like friendship and family, are confined to a private reserve. We are convinced that we do not have to stay in a place to sustain them. We tend to worry, in contrast, that our lives will become stagnant. We move forward and up. The average duration that an American home owner will stay in a home before selling and buying a better house or simply relocating is eight years. Two years is the average for renters. It would be interesting to measure how long the average friendship lasts. By "lasting friendships" I do not mean our ability to keep up with old friends by "catching up" now and then (by phone or e-mail). By friendship, I am referring to our day-to-day time spent with friends who share our lives and a common vision of what is good. Given the very structure of our lives, it is obvious why automobile manufacturers are able to advertise cars as refuges of solitude and retreat from the hustle and bustle of the world. Rest itself must be on the move.

The imperial economy is constantly on the move. New markets and new places for the economy to move must be created. There must always be a frontier waiting to be colonized in an economic sense. Both President Clinton and President Bush lobbied and pressured to give China "most favored nation" status as a trading partner. Why? China has enormous potential in the market as a nation of producers and consumers. How could China be honored with such a privilege given our concerns for oppression under its communist rule and its human rights violations? The answer given by both Democratic and Republican administrations is that the best way to change Chinese values, to interject values of democratic freedoms and individual rights, is through the market. The marketplace, free trade, the choices, products, and advertisements carry who we are, and when the imperial economy takes up residence in a place (whether in suburban Maryland or Beijing), it will somehow take control.

2

Contractual Connections and Our Economic Logic

■ Schenectady (pop. 62,000) is a moderately sized town in upstate New York. It is like many towns in the Northeast inasmuch as it reached the peak of its prosperity shortly after World War II and has declined steadily (with some ups and downs) since the end of the 1950s. I am introducing this town, rather than others, only because I spent much of the 1990s living and working in its neighbor, New York's capital city of Albany. The rise and fall of Albany corresponds a great deal to Schenectady: the loss of key manufacturing jobs and the flight of people and commerce to the suburbs and to suburban shopping malls. A similar story can be told about my own hometown, Chicopee, Massachusetts, which also peaked in the 1940s and 50s. I dwell on Schenectady because of its deep connection to a single company, General Electric. In the 1990s, GE experienced tremendous growth. It is currently one of the largest corporations in the U.S. and in the world. Although the 1990s were years of expansion for GE, it seemed that about every few months the local newspaper would announce more layoffs at the Schenectady plant and offices.

For years, every series of layoffs was met with surprise and dismay. In the mid 1940s GE employed over 40,000 workers in Schenectady; by 1990, just about 15,000; and ten years later employment hovered around 4,400. Over ten thousand jobs were lost in ten years, and every announcement of layoffs was received by shocked citizens, "Another 300 jobs? Gone?" Schenectady's mayor, Al Jurczynski, represented the town well. It was obvious that he went through various stages of mourning with each round of layoffs. He was raised in a GE family, and his brothers were still holding on to their jobs. He was dedicated to GE; the town was dedicated to GE. The company was part of the fabric of their lives. Some jobs were lost to new technology; that is understandable. But many production jobs were transferred to other parts of the country and the world, either through outsourcing (the wave of the 1990s) or in alternative GE plants in locations with less labor costs and less restrictive laws. Under its CEO, Jack Welch, GE was on the move.

Being an outsider and too young to understand, I was surprised by the mayor's shock. By the third or fourth round of layoffs, I thought that it was clear what GE was doing. Couldn't Mayor Jurczynski see it? How could he still be surprised? Now I understand. I think that I understand now for two reasons. Since then I have been raising a family, and I have been working at a single institution for a number of years. I understand that deep attachments are formed little by little and day by day. Schenectady and its mayor were not shocked about the information of more layoffs. Rather, they were taking a shock to the system, a blow to the body. They were losing part of themselves. And to make matters worse, GE was no sinking ship. The company was leaving them because it was dedicated to its shareholders, to increased profits, and to its future in the global economy. By 2002, Mayor Jurczynski had come to terms with it all—with the jilting by GE. "You have to take a reality check," he admits about his hopes for keeping GE jobs. "That's not the way corporate American operates today and that's not a slight against GE. That's just the cold, hard facts."

I have told the story of Schenectady in order to illustrate the contrast between the personal connection and loss of Mayor Jurczynski and "the cold, hard facts." The mayor was not merely losing jobs for his city; he represented the longtime citizens of Schenectady in their history, identity, and personal loss. Schenectady would have stayed with GE during hard times, but GE was giving the town hard times not in order to survive but to pursue an even better future. These are the facts about the way good business works. Manufacturing and commerce establishes and fosters certain kinds of connections, but to do good business these attachments must be maintained at a superficial level. They should be useful and productive, nothing more. The manufacturing plant will give individual employees a yearly contract, but it will not make a promise to a city to limit or to share its future. Al Jurczynski's family had shared its future with GE, and after ten thousand layoffs in ten years, the mayor had to learn not to take GE's business strategies personally.

The modern corporation operates with an impersonal logic of usefulness. The logic of the market is built into both our economic and political frameworks of competing interests and contractual commitments. Our economic and social world is a field of competing interests, where each of us is pursuing what is good for each of us. In order to advance our interests, we compete with and make coalitions between individuals, groups, companies, or whatever social unit can be understood to assert its own interests. When our interests are not opposed, we can be useful to each other. There is nothing wrong with usefulness. On the contrary, it is essential to a meaningful life that we have opportunity to be useful and to have a purpose in another person's life and in the life of institutions. In the pages of Schenectady's *Daily Gazette*, Mayor Jurczynski can be found mourning for a relationship of purpose. Schenectady wanted desperately to be useful to GE.

Our dominant forms of economic and social life require superficial attachments not because they are useful, but because they advance diverse and opposing interests, goals, and goods. It is wise to secure our interests by establishing contracts with others, but it is unwise to bind ourselves to another individual's good. Contracts are useful because they are limited in scope, established for a particular service or investment and for a restricted period of time. Through contractual agreements we share interests, but we share a deeper awareness that our overall or ultimate goals may be opposed. This narrow logic of usefulness is not reserved for corporations and commerce. It is how we operate in politics and how many of us approach friendship, marriage, neighborhoods, and church.

Few of us intend for our attachments to be short-lived, but change and independence are the order of things. Detachment is understood as freedom. It is important to be able to move on when we think necessary and to shop around. We meet people, share activities and interests, and become friends. Then, once our lives have changed (place, job, or phase of life), we either let the friendships fade or work very hard to maintain them. I dare say that I cannot claim an active friendship with an old friend if we have to coordinate our calendars months in advance. The need to schedule in a visit or to call long distance periodically is evidence that he or she is no longer a lively part of my life. Certainly there is nothing wrong with old friends, except that we Americans accrue a lot of them. An active friendship turns out to be just a stage. Most couples who live together actually stay together for only a few years. Many couples promise to stay by each other's side for a lifetime, but if their relationship lasts a decade, they have done an extraordinary thing. The average tenure in a full-time job, for Americans 35 to 44 years old, is five years. These are the cold, hard facts.

In their study, *Habits of the Heart,* Robert Bellah and a team of sociologists discovered that Americans have a difficult time trying to explain their commitments. Most in American culture think that a deep detachment from others is necessary in order to achieve autonomy, independence, success, and happiness. Certainly many people participate in common life and contribute a great deal. However, most explain their commitments through what Robert Bellah calls utilitarian and expressive individualism. The utilitarian will explain his marriage, family life, church attendance, work in the PTA, and investment in little league baseball as useful for pursuing what he thinks will make him happy. For instance, Bellah tells the story of a man who reevaluated his priorities after a divorce. In his second marriage, he decided to make family a priority not because there is anything necessary or essentially good about family, but because he realized family is a useful investment. With this kind of attachment, it is likely that he might grow out of family and shift his personal investments to other kinds of assets.

Likewise, the expressive individualist invests in community, family, and various others institutions because these groups offer opportunities for self-discovery, for an expression of one's inner self, and for developing talents and skills. Like usefulness, self-expression is a wonderful thing. We do, in fact, discover who we are through our roles and relationships with others. However, the expressivist, like the utilitarian, conceives of the self in private and individualistic terms. According to the expressivist, we find ourselves through our ability to be detached and to attach ourselves only when such attachments (like contracts) are advantageous to us. Relationships, commitments, roles, and responsibilities are understood as impermanent phases of life. We get what we can out of various people, places, and stages of life, with the assumption that we will one day have to move on to a different phase of our development and self-discovery.

In order to become an adult we must leave home. We must put the values in which we were raised at a distance, at least for a time. From a distance we can evaluate their merit, and then, if they hold up, we can call these values our own. Note that "values" is a useful economic term, by which we are able to judge the cost and benefits of moral claims and then invest in them if we desire to do so. To be an adult, we need to "buy into" and possess our own personal view of life. It is commonly assumed that we are diminished when we say, "I never questioned but simply accepted the values with which I was raised." In order to have mature faith we must evaluate various alternatives, leave the church in which we were raised, and decide for ourselves whether or not it is good for us to return. We Americans like to construct our lives from the ground up, beginning with our detachment from others, attaining mature independence and self-reliance, and then settling in (for a time) in the kind of life we can call our own. We start new families, choose our values and then cooperate with others who share them, and feel the pain of moving past phases of life that begin to hold us back. We are on the move.

3

Friendship

■ An alternative to the disengagement of self-making is friendship. Friendships come in many different shapes, sizes, and colors. The word "friend" seems to be used with as much variety as the word "love," as in "I love my husband," "I love pizza," and "I love that shirt." I suppose that we will call another person a friend, at least in a very broad sense, when we share time with one another and hold warm regard for each other. I am referring here to friendship that is based in friendliness. It seems right to call a coworker or neighbor a friend if she has been sociable and receptive, and if she has not done anything to be called an adversary. For this reason, dogs are wonderful friends. It does not make sense to befriend pizza or a nice-looking shirt, but dogs will do. They are sociable and responsive; they affectionately and faithfully stay by our sides. Dogs are loved as friends because they offer a good measure of return—a relationship that is not experienced in relation to pizza or a shirt. Even though friendships come in many forms, the idea of friendship says something distinctive about relationships of love. There is giving and receiving. There is something to share.

Jack McCarthy, age three, knows the wonder and pain of friendship. He spends his preschool days at home, and he cries when his brother and sister leave him and go off to school. He does not want to go with them. In fact, after a few weeks at a half-day preschool, Jack announced that he was through with school—not just through with the year or with preschool, but with all of his schooling. He has dropped out of school for good. He's done, and he wants his older sister and brother home with him. He does not want to join them at some unfamiliar place. The reason is clear. Abby and Quin, together, have a great capacity and authority of imagination. They are the necessary supports for the world where Jack wants to dwell.

Abby, Quin, and Jack together can see and act in their shared world. Jack's nine-month-old brother is also part of it, but his mother and I are strangers. We cannot reproduce their shared world even if we (halfheartedly) try. We simply do not know the nuances and the feel. I only witness children barking like dogs, or spying on me and sneaking around and under furniture, or battling dark forces, constructing mansions, castles, and dungeons, or drifting at sea upon the good ship sofa. Sometimes I am instructed to take in and feed four orphans. I do. On other occasions I suspect that I am an ogre or troll. If I am lucky, I am a grandfather who has the good pleasure of entertaining his grandchildren when they arrive in the kitchen for a snack.

When Jack's companions go off to school this wonderful world is lost to him. He cannot sustain it alone. Because it is so rich and lively, it is not a world that can be sustained alone by anyone. When his brother and sister are gone, Jack waits impatiently for their return. When they do return he will end up fighting and arguing with them. Good friends do not always agree. He will have to work hard to negotiate his role and the nature of the world they will inhabit (after all, he is younger than they are). It will not be easy, but it will be their world. When his brother and sister return from school, he will finally have, in his words, "something to do."

This "shared world" and "something to do" are at the heart of friendship. In a very serious way, friends help each other to see the world and to act in it. Good friends share a vision of what is real and true, and they share a course of action and a journey toward what is true and good. Merely "convenient" or "handy" friendships share one or two common interests, and a useful relationship for attaining the interests. This too is a shared perspective, albeit a narrow one. For instance, coworkers might cooperate in work and socialize outside of work. They might enjoy each other's company a great deal. In this case they share a measure of friendship. If they become "good friends," however, they will share a conception of what is good, work toward it, and risk correcting each other when one or the other strays from the path. "That is not what *we* are about," one friend will say to the other. When we entertain only convenient or handy friends, we say to our husbands and wives, "That is not what *we* are about," with a raised eyebrow, only after the "friend" has gone home. True friendship requires not only shared time and warm regard, but a common ability to see, to judge, and to be faithful to a shared good.

In the immaturity of our children, the common vision of friendship is sometimes easier to see. This is why we parents worry about the friends of our children (whether 3 years old, 13, or 30). Our children (especially those 13 years old) do not know what the worry is all about. Through friendships we gain a sense of who we are and what the world is like—of who we are in the world. In a very concrete sense, our friends constitute the universe of the everyday, and they become part of how we experience good things and bad in the course of the day. We share colloquialisms and slang to describe people and events. We might not always agree, but we have a common vocabulary and a means to communicate to our friends what is important in the world around us. Through our day-to-day interchanges we share a place in the world.

Our daughter is in second grade, but already my wife, Bridget, and I see that some of Abigail's friends are better for her than others. She already has to negotiate the schoolyard terrain of "if you are her friend, you cannot be mine." Some "friends" make unreasonable demands; some put her on edge. Already, she has schoolmates who see the world through cell phones and Britney Spears. We say that these classmates are not good for her. We mean that they offer Abigail a perspective on the world that subverts our homespun world of *Mary Poppins* and "a spoon full of sugar." Britney is on the attack. She is everywhere. Abigail and Quin have been singing a refrain from one of her songs, "I'm not that innocent." Our seven-year-old girl dances about singing, "I'm not that innocent." Then her little brother will appear in order to ask what "innocent" means. Do I tell him that Britney is saying that she is guilty or worldly? I do not like the question. I do not know what the song is about, and I do not want to know. It represents a kind of subversion brought on by the world that Abigail receives through her friends at school.

Friendship is disruptive. I do not mean friendliness and sociability, which function to keep life steady and smooth. Friendliness is the American way of making contact without getting close; it keeps our divergent attitudes and conceptions about life from causing trouble. Friendship, in contrast, requires an intimacy where we imagine a common future and sustain a common "world." Because friends go after something together, they seldom worry about "niceties" and friendliness with each other. Politeness is a concern with strangers, while "getting it right" is the concern among friends.

Good friends join together in a common vision that outsiders sometimes consider elitist, exclusive, a threat, or just difficult to understand. I have the clear sense of being an outsider when I first encounter a very hospitable group of people who are already good friends. Someone will refer to a name or a place, a person or an event, and a memory will be conjured up. Some in the circle of friends will grin; some will cringe, and it is clear that I have missed something. An ungracious group will be indifferent to my confusion. They may even take a bit of silent joy in the recognition that they have a bond that I do not share. My exclusion confirms their bond. Their friendship is sustained with a slightly more sophisticated version of the schoolyard declaration, "If you are her friend, you cannot be mine." Their friendship seems to establish itself in opposition to other groups.

On the other hand, when a hospitable circle sees that I have been left out, one of the friends will stop for a moment in order to explain. In fact, explaining their common memory will be a pleasure because the friends will have a chance to dwell on their common life and to invite another person in. They will dispute the details, and I will probably receive four different accounts of the same event. They will argue with each other, but they show patience with me. They want to "get it right" for me. Their hospitality to me has been an occasion to remember important events in their common life. Like the inhospitable group, this gracious and open set of friendships is disruptive. The inhospitable group sets itself apart from common life in general, but the hospitable group is far more danger-ous. When matched with their constant openness to others, their intense friendship threatens to subvert other "common visions" and "common worlds." They will try to befriend me, and if I join the circle of friends—as an equal among them—their friendship will dominate my time.

New and enlivening friendships may threaten our old world, introduc-ing into our homes a slightly more sophisticated version of the intru-sion of Britney Spears. After Britney's lyrics, our family may never sing "A Spoon Full of Sugar" again. I should admit that I often think about hospitable friendships much the same as I do Britney Spears. When I encounter a tight circle of friends, I am usually "turned off" by them. If they want to explain their inside jokes, I am not seriously interested. I am likely to laugh, but I do not want to go further into their world. The more they persist, the more likely I am to become annoyed with their joy in each other. I will guess that their friendships are really just contrived and superficial—"put on" like a show. I will consider them pushy. If they continue with their overtures of friendship, I will withdraw. I must refuse. Don't they understand that I have a life of my own? I'm busy, and I don't have time for a whole new life.

For this reason, closed friendships are upsetting initially because they do not offer friendliness to outsiders, but open friendships are far more disruptive because they invite outsiders in. Life at work, in the neighbor-hood, at home, in the schoolyard, or among our best companions and allies might go on smoothly and in a friendly way without the intrusion of friendships. Friendliness is safe and stable, and therefore more com-mon and acceptable than captivating friendships. Lively friendships form

36

when two or three in the neighborhood or workplace start thinking and seeing things together. They start talking and become captivated by an idea or vision of what they can do and where they can go together. They will begin to form a place in the world together that is deeper and richer than it is when each goes about his or her business alone.

Friends start to do more than just spend time or cooperate at work. They start to live, struggle, and move forward side by side with the same way of envisioning the future. Friends conspire. They plan. They want to make a difference. They seek a goal that is beyond each and attainable only together. Together, they are able to imagine a different kind of world, and together they are able to act in it. Such friendship can be closed in upon itself or open to any who are captivated by the same journey. Friendship brings either withdrawal or an offer that will change us. When friendship brings an offer of hospitality, it is an intrusion upon our safe and smooth-running world.

4

God's Gift of Friendship

■ "This is my commandment, that you love one another as I have loved you. No one has greater love than this, to lay down one's life for one's friends" (John 15:12–13). In Jesus Christ, God has drawn near to us with the hospitality of divine friendship. Often it seems that life would be much easier for everyone, from the perspective of day-to-day work and play, if God were distant. I have a good life and a full schedule. Just let me go about my business; I am doing just fine. From this perspective, God's hospitality is intrusive and dangerous. It is much easier to think about God as a task master or powerful monarch who is mysteriously closed to us. We can dismiss such a God. It is much easier to think about God's friendship in terms of the inhospitable, withdrawn, and self-involved sort. It is much easier to be inhospitable and withdrawn. But God's hospitality intrudes upon us.

"I do not call you servants any longer, because the servant does not know what the master is doing; but I have called you friends, because I have made known to you everything that I have heard from my Father" (John 15:15). Love one another; this is a command. We have been chosen for God's gracious friendship and appointed to go and bear fruit (v. 16). It is interesting that, in John 15:15–16, the distinction between slavery and friendship hinges on knowledge rather than freedom: "I have made known to you everything." We are receiving a command; we are not free to judge its merits, and Jesus notes that we do not have opportunity to choose it for ourselves. We already have been chosen. God has taken the first step. When we are called friends of God, the emphasis is not on our own achievement—not on our ability to attain the status of God's friend through the power of our choices. The emphasis is on common knowledge, on sharing a common vision, on seeing the world from God's point of view. God's invitation of friendship, in Jesus Christ, offers a share in God's way of knowing the world, of seeing and acting in it, of imagining its present and future in God's love. It is striking to me how wonderful this invitation is, but also how intrusive and disruptive it is likely to appear.

The Gospel of John begins with the tensions created by God's offer of friendship. "In the beginning was the Word" (1:1), and "all things came into being through him" (1:3). "He was in the world, and the world came into being through him; yet the world did not know him. He came to what was his own, and his own people did not accept him" (John 1:10–11). It would be easy to interpret "his own people" narrowly as "the Jews," who are frequently mentioned in John's Gospel. But in doing so, we will miss the point as it applies more broadly to us and to the world. "The Jews" in the Gospel of John are God's people. We share the same position as "the Jews" when we Christians call upon God in worship. According to John 1:10–11, God comes to what is already his own, and by and large we do not appreciate having to turn the world back over to him. If there is an intrusion in the world, it is on our side of things, for we are the guests. We are the cliquish friends who have withdrawn, who have the inside jokes, and who carry on in self-satisfaction with our own little games.

There is not just one game in the world. There are many ways that human beings withdraw and divide up the world: into the good and bad, rich and poor, in and out of step. We have our own games—we upwardly mobile Americans—those of us imbued with the logic of contracts, convenience, and efficiency, with moving on, with personal growth, with cost-benefit analyses, and with mere friendliness. God's friendship is dangerous to us because it undermines our handy friendships and ways of detachment, and, in the process, it undermines the manner in which we are attached to the world. If we have been setting out to find ourselves through following our own way and building our own futures, God's friendship undermines our identities and the vision of the world that we call our own.

In Philippians 2, Paul indicates that our "sharing in the Spirit" comes to its fulfillment when we share the love and mind of Christ:

Let the same mind be in you that was in Christ Jesus,
who, though he was in the form of God, did not regard equality with
God as something to be exploited,

but emptied himself, taking the form of a slave, being born in human
   likeness.
And being found in human form, he humbled himself and became obe-
   dient to the point of death—even death on a cross.
Therefore God also highly exalted him and gave him the name that is
   above every name,
so that at the name of Jesus every knee should bend, in heaven and on
   earth and under the earth,
and every tongue should confess that Jesus Christ is Lord, to the glory
   of God the Father.

Philippians 2:5–11

Paul cites this hymn to Christ like the preacher that he is. He exhorts the Christians in Philippi to recognize the gift of God's love for us—the kind of love where one does "nothing from selfish ambition or conceit." He calls them not only to acknowledge the gift but to live it, to be bound to each other with it, to think, see, and act toward each other with the mind and love of Christ.

The structure of this hymn is important. Jesus is humbled by human powers that lord over him with the sentence of death. He is humbled by the cross, which was not only a way of putting people to death but also a sign of the imperial power of Rome. The Romans make an example of him. His crucifixion, like that of other Jews in the empire, is a visible assertion of a kingdom's reign. Jesus does not claim his "equality with God" by crushing the powers of the world. He does not respond to the world with its own power to mete out death, and for this Jesus is exalted, and all in heaven and on earth should bow. The cross of Christ becomes the sign of an entirely different lordship in the reign of the kingdom of God.

The king of kings reigns through peace, and the appropriate response to this self-giving love of God is worship. We bend our knees not to Caesar, not to an untouchable power who rules by force and the threat of force, but to God who offers the grace and friendship of sharing in the divine life and participating in God's way in the world. The appropriate response to the Lord who befriends all of creation is to bow *with* all of heaven and earth, to hear the groaning of creation and to see the desires of men and women as the thirst for divine love. The appropriate response to God's friendship is, in the words of St. Thomas Aquinas, to be friends of God's friends.

The center point of our friendship with God is corporate worship. Gathered for worship, the church is God's sign of friendship with the world. The church is the body of Christ. Go to a church as it prays and look around. You will see it, the subversive friendship of God's hospitality. You will see Pharisees congratulating themselves for their own

40

righteousness. You will see tax collectors and those who cheat on their income taxes. You will see sinners. You will see many saints, but you will also see adulterers, thieves, liars, petty embezzlers, and colossal hypocrites. You will see elderly folk and kids who misbehave. You will see the kind of people whom God has befriended. This is no photo-op with the president. It is not lunch with the CEO. The church is not the kind of gathering that bodes well for running an efficient corporation or effective government. It is not the kind of gathering that many think is most valuable for church growth or for the proper political or social mission of the church in the world. However, it is precisely the kind of gathering that represents God's people. This is Christ's body and the sign of God's offer of friendship with the world.

What are these people qualified to do together except worship? They can gather, confess their sins, ask for God's mercy, and be changed by God's friendship. They can hear the word of the Bible and God's story told. They can share the gift of God's presence. They can break bread and drink from the cup of the crucifixion. They can be bound to each other and take possession of the world by God's grace and peace. They can be a people who live by God's disruptive hospitality, always open to an expanding circle of friends.

5

Love and Justice

■ Although the title is "Love and Justice," the topic of this chapter is "taking possession." I was tempted with titles like "Taking Possession" or "Staking a Claim," but I had second thoughts about causing confusion. These titles sound too much like the logic of an economy that requires ever-greater consumption and means of acquisition. Our modern growth economy requires that our attachments to people and things be superficial. We must be on the move in order to follow the market. We must be detached in order to find ourselves by passing through friendships, family, and phases of life. We must be independent and self-sustaining. The friendship of God—being friends of God's friends—is *the* alternative to this restlessness of the world and our longing for freedom. It is the freedom of God's communion. Friendship in God's name is an alternative venture, a different way of staking a claim.

"Blessed are the poor in spirit, for theirs is the kingdom of heaven" (Matt. 5:3). Those who know the weight of a heavy spirit and the great distance of God's ways from our own will take possession of heaven. "Blessed are the meek, for they will inherit the earth" (Matt. 5:5). Those who patiently wait and hope for mercy and grace, who are last in the land grab, they will take ownership of the earth. These beatitudes are not imperatives. They do not *command* that we *should be* poor in spirit or meek. Rather, they are statements of fact. They are counterfactual declarations about ownership and "taking possession" in our world. There are many ways in our world to seek satisfaction and fulfillment. A nice car and house will help for a time, but among the many ways of desiring and striving for our good and good things, it will be those who hunger and thirst for righteousness who will be satisfied (Matt. 5:6). It is those who mourn who will be given comfort and strength. It is the merciful who will receive mercy. The rest will continue to be restless. Only God's friendship fulfills.

By calling the chapter "Love and Justice," I propose that we return to the contrast between the dependence of Schenectady's citizens upon General Electric and "the cold, hard facts." The facts, in this case, are that GE owes Schenectady nothing. No injustice is done when a business moves its jobs and shifts its alliances to a more profitable place. That is the way that we divide the world between love and justice: love is workable among family and friends, while justice is a matter of impersonal rights and duties. In the usual process of justice, we are not bound to others and to their good. Justice, we assume, allows us to be useful to each other, whether allies or strangers. Justice is what we deserve and what we owe. Love is a gift.

Certainly love and justice have different ends. Love is directed to our union with others, while justice settles accounts. Love sustains empathy, self-giving, and union. Love offers a deep sense of being together that is far deeper than usefulness and merit. Through love our relationships are elevated beyond self-interest and self-directed needs. In contrast, justice allows us to determine what we owe so that we can repay. Justice binds through impersonal obligations and remunerations, through duties and rights.

However, even though they have distinct ways of holding us together, love and justice are not opposed. It might be argued that great injustices in the world are caused by the very alienation of justice from love. Love requires justice; it requires that we see the people we love "on their own merit" and give them what they deserve. When we find ourselves "in the middle of things," justice opens a way for love. However, it is love that is the beginning and the end.

Through justice, a transaction or agreement might be finished, but the relationship is left incomplete. In the give and take of life, justice provides a means of evening the score, paying off our debts, and receiving what we deserve. Yet, in the give and take of duties and rights, even with what we owe and what we deserve from strangers, we will find that we are never "even." When we treat each other with justice, we are directed to calling each other friends—to sharing a vision of what is right and good. In other words, it is GE that is mistaken about the facts. The company's give and take with generations of workers and citizens has created deep connections and shared goods. Going about our business with people is not a simple matter. Call an electrician once, and you will receive a service. Call the same electrician several times over a number of years, and he is your electrician, and your wiring is his. He may drink your coffee, and he will certainly ask about your children. Justice is completed in the gift.

In order to keep justice from binding us to people, either superficial interaction or injustice is necessary. By superficial interaction I do not mean harm or evil, but simply a brief exchange with a cashier at the grocery store. By injustice, I do mean some kind of wrong done, one that will help bring a deeper habit of interaction to an end. When relationships reach any kind of depth, justice will bind us with the imperative of love.

This claim about love and justice is opposed to the usual interpretation of Jesus' parable of the dishonest steward (Luke 16:1–9). As the customary reading goes, a dishonest use of money makes good friends. The parable begins with the steward's dishonesty. Word of his schemes and carelessness has reached his employer, who calls him to give account of his dealings. He has been caught squandering his master's wealth, but he is clever. "Summoning his master's debtors one by one, he asked the first, 'How much do you owe my master?' He answered, 'A hundred jugs of olive oil.' He said to him, 'Take your bill, sit down quickly, and make it fifty.'" The manager does the same with the others. The bill for one hundred containers of wheat becomes a bill for eighty, and so on. When the master hears of his servant's course of action, he commends the dishonest steward for his cunning. The lesson of the parable: "the children of this age are more shrewd in dealing with their own generation than are the children of light. . . . make friends for yourselves by means of dishonest wealth so that when it is gone, they may welcome you into the eternal homes" (16:8–9).

In the usual interpretation, the dishonest servant makes friends by cheating his master further, and, oddly, the master honors him for it. A bit of information about the customary bill of sale puts the parable in a different, more sensible light. J. Duncan Derrett, a historian of ancient law, claims that it was regular practice among faithful Jews to falsify a bill of sale in order to circumvent the biblical law against charging interest. If I were to allow you to make use of my property with the arrangement of full payment at a later time, I could not, according to Jewish law, charge you interest (as we now do for such things as automobiles and couches). However, I could get around the letter of the law by writing out a bill of sale for a $10,000 car, when in fact an $8,000 one was purchased. Both buyer and seller would be pleased. The buyer owns a car without cash in hand, and the seller is compensated accordingly. With this ancient practice in mind, the parable reads differently. If our dishonest steward is allowing a debtor to redraft his debt from 100 to 80 bails of wheat, he is not cheating his master further, but realigning his master's commerce to accord with biblical law. This is how the clever steward makes friends; he makes good on formerly dishonest wealth.

The clever steward sees that in order to befriend his employer's clients he must deal with them justly. His actions are not much different from the surprising turnaround of Zacchaeus, the tax collector who gives back to the poor and pledges no longer to defraud anyone (Luke 19:1–10). There is a simple lesson in the parable of the dishonest steward: make friends by dealing justly with others. It is striking how often people lie, misrepresent, and falsify their dealings not in order to cheat others for profit but in order to make and keep friends. The little lies I might tell my sister are for her own good, to make her happy, or to protect her from needless anxiety. The lies that we tell together protect our shared good. Little falsehoods keep us together and keep others in the dark. The more our friendships require falsehoods, the more we will need to solidify our common bonds by turning against enemies and shutting out strangers. The strangeness of God's justice, in contrast, always threatens to pull us into God's love, where we come to call adversaries our friends.

Consider the parable of the vineyard (Matt. 20:1–16). A landowner hires laborers at the beginning of a day's harvest, and they agree upon a day's wage. Throughout the day the vineyard owner goes out to the town square and hires more workers, until the last set joins the harvest for only one hour. These last are paid a full day's wage, and when those who actually worked a full day receive the same wage, they are angry. "So the last will be first, and the first will be last" (20:16). This is not fair. Anyone who worked all day would be angry. I would be furious. I would take exception—unless of course one of the workers who labored for an hour was a dear friend. I would have been worrying about him all day. Is he still in town waiting to be hired? He needs work desperately. I know his situation; he must be pacing nervously, eager to take any kind of work. Finally, when I see that he has arrived at the vineyard, even at the last hour, I am happy. When he receives a full day's wage, I am overjoyed. I love him as a brother, and I would gladly work all day so that each of us can put food on the table.

The owner of the vineyard commits no injustice, and those who had labored all day would see the good of his actions if the last workers were their friends. We would see that they have been waiting anxiously and hoping against hope to be hired. Imagine their joy when they were hired as the sun was beginning to set. Imagine their joy at a day's wage. God's justice is strange to the world because we are asked not only to give others what they deserve but also to see them as our friends because they are friends of God.

6

God and Neighbor

■ The parable of the Good Samaritan (Luke 10:29–37) is central to how Christians understand love of neighbor. The parable is the parable of "being a friend of God's friends." The story that Jesus tells is initiated by a lawyer's question, "What must I do to inherit eternal life?" (10:25). Jesus responds by asking the lawyer about the law, and the lawyer responds with the dual commands of loving God totally and in every respect, and loving one's neighbor as one's self. "Do this, and you will live," Jesus replies, and then he tells the story of the Good Samaritan in order to answer the lawyer's follow-up question, "Who is my neighbor?" In my review of this parable I will dwell on two important details. The first is the ordinary nature of the Samaritan's actions, and the second is the contrast between the unreserved love of God (with all your heart, soul, and strength) and the conditions of neighborly love (that is, love him or her as you love yourself).

The Good Samaritan gives aid to a man, presumably a Jewish man, who was traveling from Jerusalem to Jericho and was attacked, robbed, and left on the roadside half dead. As the parable unfolds, the Samaritan's assistance to the man becomes remarkable through its contrast to the actions of more distinguished characters of the story. A priest and a Levite see the beaten man and disregard his plight. They are on their way to Jerusalem. Presumably, they have religious duties that would be disturbed, delayed, or undermined by contact with the beaten and bloodied man. Jesus' parable leads the lawyer to conclude that the neighbor to the injured man was "the one who showed him mercy" (Luke 10:37).

The neighbor is the Samaritan. His actions are certainly gracious and

46

good, but not extraordinary. Have we become so callused and self-serving that we find the Samaritan's actions amazing or self-sacrificial? Do we believe that his actions have transcended what justice requires? I hope not. The surprise for the lawyer is not the actions of mercy, but the combination of what is done and who does it. Who is my neighbor whom I am called to love as myself? It is not so much the distinguished priest or Levite as the despised Samaritan. He is one of those apostates to the north who worship in the wrong place and in the wrong way yet claim a pedigree and place before God equal to our own. He is an outsider who claims to be better than us. To this degree, if the Samaritan is the good neighbor, he is first of all the lawyer's rival. "If you love those who love you, what credit is that to you?" (Luke 6:32). "But love your enemies, do good, and lend, expecting nothing in return. Your reward will be great, and you will be children of the Most High; for he is kind to the ungrateful and the wicked. Be merciful, just as your Father is merciful" (Luke 6:35–36).

On January 11, 2003, two days before leaving office, Republican governor George Ryan angered and betrayed many and delighted some when he commuted the death sentences for every condemned prisoner in the state of Illinois. I was told that the *Oprah* show sent its camera crews to the living rooms of several angry and distressed families. I read similar coverage on the front page of the *Washington Post* (January 14, 2003). Tim Barton was interviewed. In 1988, his sweetheart was brutally and randomly murdered by one of the death row inmates, who now will serve life in prison. In the article Barton tells his story of loss and his desire for justice. He accuses Governor Ryan of "playing God . . . from a constitutional point of view." His loved one is gone. He admits that capital punishment will offer revenge, and he demands it. Everything has been taken from his beloved, and her killer "can survive and have some status or strive for some status in that community [in a maximum security prison]." Barton admits a profound sense of helplessness. Without the death penalty, he believes that any measure of justice and closure has been taken away from him.

To love your neighbor as yourself is, indeed, a hard lesson, and in Barton's case, one that violates justice. I imagine that the death row inmate has a father, mother, sister, and brother who believe that the governor's mercy has brought justice and that life in prison is what their son and brother deserves, perhaps even what he needs. What would I want for my son if he were a murderer? What would I want for a murderer if my wife were killed? These are difficult questions to answer. The victim's family or the murderer's family: whose judgment is clouded? Who sees the murderer for who he is and his horrible acts in their proper light? Is he evil or is he good? Certainly, the judgment of justice is a matter of perspective. This is why justice requires our judgments. In order to gain perspective, I suggest that we begin with how we are supposed to see ourselves.

The love of self is often understood in a trivial sense—represented by the popularity of Whitney Houston's rendition of "The Greatest Love of All." The song is decades old, but its message is as popular as ever. In a popular view, we love ourselves by affirming who we are, having a sense of pride, being our own heroes, walking in no one's shadow, and depending only on ourselves. This is the greatest love of all. Obviously, the song is corny, but it does reflect a higher-minded view about the modern self. When I look inwardly at who I am, I am all that I see. I am who I have; I am who I am. The Christian faith gives us a different picture of the self. When we look inward, we see God with us.

In telling the story of his life, St. Augustine describes how God had been drawing him near at every turn and path, even when he had been turning away from God. He looks back at his life of confident misunderstandings about the world and even about his own motives and desires. In looking back at his own searching for God, he realizes that God had been working deep within him and for him all along. This recognition brings a liberating kind of surrender and obedience. According to our faith, God's movement within us is not a challenge to our free will. On the contrary, when we resist God's friendship, we lessen ourselves and inhibit our freedom to be fulfilled and completed in the good—the Good who is the very God who befriends us. God's grace does not limit us, but restores us inwardly, which means that we are restored outwardly in the love of God and neighbor. In our freedom to turn away from God, we become slaves to ourselves (and we are likely to enslave others as well). When we look inwardly and see ourselves truthfully, we see that the independent and autonomous self is alienated from itself and that we "come into ourselves" through communion with God. When we look at ourselves through the eyes of faith, we see a desire for fulfillment through our good actions and bad. We see our restlessness. We may see our frustrated efforts to be our own heroes and depend only on ourselves, but we will also see God's patient and liberating grace.

To love God with all my heart, soul, and strength is to love myself in the fullest, and to love my neighbor as myself is to love another as fully loved by God. There is no one beyond God's mercy and ever-present love. This offer of love is God's justice. To see what we owe to our neighbor, we depend upon God's grace. We need the eyes of faith, the patience that comes with hope, and the courage that is required of love. And our biblical faith does not stop there. When we follow Jesus, we are called to go where he goes and to see and make judgments about the world from a particular place. We are called to see our Lord in the faces of the hungry and thirsty, in the sojourner who needs hospitality, in those who need a coat and shirt, in the sick, and in the imprisoned (Matt. 25:31–46). If we can see God there, we can know the love of God, love of neighbor, and love of self.

7

Family First

■ Our first neighbors are the members of our families. There are many kinds of families and ways that one becomes part of a family. A person may have been adopted or brought up in a group home. One might be part of a stable nuclear family or an equally constant household of grandparents, uncles, and aunts. Many are reared by a single parent. In the U.S., many children are raised in what are called "combined" families, where a husband and wife combine children of previous marriages. Some are raised in a series of family groupings: first in a nuclear family, then with a single parent, afterward in a combined family, and perhaps in a single-parent household again. In Western cultures generally, an increasing amount of couples are attempting to live together and to raise children apart from marriage. The prospects for those who "live together" are not promising. Most of these unions dissolve after a few years, which means that the meaning of family is even more variable and elusive.

Family is vital to personal identity and moral formation. We all need a context of relationships where we are nurtured, protected, and educated. We need folk with whom we are at home, who are looking out for our good. We need a place where we do not need an invitation—a place with others that is our own, where we do not have to knock or announce our entry. Pope John Paul II calls the family the "genealogy of the person." In other words, we trace the lineage of our character and habits, as well as our capacity for love and friendship, through our formation and struggles in family. Relationships of home, in other words, are the context for the genesis of personhood.

Given the importance of family, the various derivations and deviations of the modern household are cause for concern. For more than a few decades, family has been a battleground and source of agitation for social critics, commentators, politicians, and members of the PTA. We all should worry that many children are neglected and abused at home. We should be concerned for all our children. We should worry also that our habits of dividing, dissolving, and combining families cultivate an identity of detachment and impermanence. Our identities, like the ever-changing shape of family, may begin to appear arbitrary and provisional. We should worry as well that people might learn indifference and self-satisfaction at home. For some, family is a private fortress with walls that shield its members from the worries of the world. We should worry that our best homes provide only a refuge for their members. We should worry when families attempt to shield their sons and daughters from all the pains and troubles of the world, and that no expense is spared for their private success and individual well-being. We should worry, in this case, that the home has turned inward, and that family has become a private (and ironically individualistic) concern.

Jesus has a mixed record on family. Certainly he welcomes the children, but in Luke 14:26 his words are harsh, "Whoever comes to me and does not hate father and mother, wife and children, brothers and sisters, yes, and even life itself, cannot be my disciple." In Matthew 10, Jesus offers an equally severe challenge, "For I have come to set a man against his father, and a daughter against her mother, . . . and one's foes will be members of one's own household" (vv. 35–36). In the next verse, the meaning of this challenge is explained, "Whoever loves father or mother more than me is not worthy of me; and whoever loves son or daughter more than me is not worthy of me" (Matt. 10:37). This passage indicates that "hating" one's father or mother is an exaggeration for purposes of emphasis and rhetorical effect. Obviously, we are not called to hate, but to love. We need not despise our parents if we love God above all.

Although Jesus' challenge to family can be explained, we ought not to disregard the hyperbolic "hate" too easily. The verses in Matthew 10:35–36 are cited from Micah 7:6. Micah is a prophet who (around 700 B.C.) announces God's judgment against the idolatry and unfaithfulness of Israel as well as God's promise of forgiveness and restoration. When Micah denounces the corruption of Israel, he uses the inner strife of family as clear evidence of their unfaithfulness. "The faithful have disappeared from the land" (7:2), and "the best of them is like a brier, the most upright of them a thorn hedge" (v. 4). Micah advises the people to "put no trust in a friend, have no confidence in a loved one; . . . for the son

50

treats the father with contempt, the daughter rises up against her mother, . . . your enemies are members of your own household" (vv. 5–6). Micah shows the folly of trust in one's kin, and calls for faith and confidence in the Lord. "But as for me, I will look to the Lord, I will wait for the God of my salvation; my God will hear me" (v. 7).

Our times are not so different. The troubles of the home and our persistent calls for a renewal of good families are both a sign. On one hand, our children are closely monitored and supported. On the other hand, they are part of a world of weapons and violence, real and imagined, feared in the streets and enjoyed on television and video games. On one hand, we dwell on the joys of marriage and good parenting. But on the other, domestic abuse and sexual violence are as common as ever. Family is the focus of both problems and solutions, and in the last few decades, defenders of family are almost everywhere. The need for strong families has become a political mantra for both conservatives and liberals. Everyone claims to be on the side of the happy home. Who would dare suggest, even in good-natured exaggeration, that one ought to hate one's father and mother? Jesus did. His teaching ought not to be explained away. For Christians, the family-first movement is wrongheaded. Certainly there is truth in the view that we are nurtured and receive our identities and dignity in family. But for Christians, our first family is not found in the private home; rather, our kinship and bonds of home are among the people of the church.

Remember that God's friendship and hospitality are disruptive. Jesus will be a guest in the home of Zacchaeus, and as a result, he, his household, and his way of doing business will never be the same. In John 14, Jesus offers an extended explanation of God's promises of fellowship with us through the glory of the Son's union with the Father. In John, Jesus turns to the metaphor of God's home. The chapter begins with reference to the many dwelling places of God's house (14:2). His promise is that we will not be left orphaned (v. 18). "Those who love me will keep my word, and my Father will love them, and we will come to them and make our home with them" (v. 23). It is God's "kinship" that will define our own.

"Who is my mother, and who are my brothers?" This seems to be a cold reply, given by Jesus when he is told that his mother and brothers are inquiring after him and waiting outside to see him. Who is my family? "And pointing to his disciples, he said, 'Here are my mother and my brothers! For whoever does the will of my Father in heaven is my brother and sister and mother'" (Matt. 12:48–50). When reflecting on this passage, Augustine attempts to understand Jesus' words as an invitation to us rather than a rejection of his family. To do so, he turns directly to Mary. He points out that Mary's relationship to the Lord, as his mother, is made possible through her acceptance and conformity to God's will. Augustine explains that Mary bears Jesus, the Son, only after she has been united with him through her assent and response of faith. Her spiritual kinship, therefore, precedes her biological motherhood. Likewise, faith determines our birthright. According to Augustine, the family that is born in Christ's Spirit comes before ties of genetic inheritance. Baptism establishes a communion that qualifies our relationships of birth. We all are adopted daughters and sons of God.

The church is our first family. Such a claim does not mean that we must leave our homes and take up a common residence. It does mean, however, that our separate homes are not independent units or autonomous domains. They are dependent and fulfilled in sharing common life with the church. We do not solve problems by striving to make our private families self-sufficient. We have a responsibility, for instance, for providing the financial resources, our time, and our hard work to sustain the church building and sanctuary. This common place is our home, and how we maintain our home ought to reflect our faith in God's hospitality. How is it possible that some churches are vacant and locked during the week? Shouldn't someone, at least one person, be home in order to entertain the unexpected guest and stranger who could be Christ? If we are worried about thieves or vandals, isn't that partly a good sign? Isn't the church, then, in the right place?

If the church is our first family, then our second homes should be defined by it, and our doors ought to be open to the stranger, the sick, and the poor. Insofar as God's hospitality defines the church, it defines our separate homes as well. It is part of the American dream to have a home that is our castle—palatial, rich in comforts, and with the modern version of a drawbridge and moat. We want a spacious yard and a long driveway to keep us from the entanglements of our neighbors. In the least, we hope to find a friendly neighborhood where we can have cookouts and share other recreational and voluntary activities. We do not want to be bound or dependent. We do not want noisy neighbors who might be knocking on our doors for a loaf of bread. If there are few knocks, isn't that a troublesome sign?

Family life, when enlivened and supported by the church, can be a venture and an invitation rather than a defense and escape. Certainly the shape of the contemporary family is troubled, varied, and inconsistent, but God's offer of kinship is already disruptive of the sheltered and self-sufficient home. It takes an enormous amount of trust and hope to turn our private families outward, but the risk can be taken if we welcome Christ into our homes. The hospitality of home requires little steps, like making a habit of inviting guests for a meal and living modestly so that we can contribute more to community life. We can shut off the television and take a walk. On the way we might develop connections and common projects with our neighbors. We might ease each other's burdens, care for the sick, visit the shut-ins, and help raise each other's children. We might develop systems for exchanging hand-me-down clothes, sports equipment, and toys. We might spend our leisure looking out for the good of our neighbors.

In day-to-day matters of life, family among Christians is not only a shared undertaking of neighbor love but also an adventure of faith in God's love. Not all of us are up to the hazards of such an adventure, and none of us can manage the risks alone. If a person does not want to risk much, she should go bungee jumping or skydiving. Although exciting, such "thrill seeking" does not require that a person give his or her life to another. Bungee jumping and skydiving are private pleasures and always a matter of personal choice. Such thrill seeking requires far less courage, faith, and hope than joining with another in marriage and together raising a family. We accept a great deal of risk when we declare that our love will endure "for richer and for poorer, in sickness and in health" and trust that God's love will see us through to the end of our days. Marriage is central to family. In order to better understand our familial bonds as children of God, it will be helpful to give marriage a closer look.

8

Marriage

■ When a couple is married, the two are often congratulated on the occasion of "starting a new family." Although well-wishers are good intentioned, their hopes for "a new family" are misplaced. If the couple is part of a community of faith, they already have been and still are connected to their adopted kin—not to mention the particular families and communities in which each was raised. Nevertheless, there is truth to the notion that something new is happening when a husband and wife take their vows. By making vows before the gathered church, a woman and man are binding themselves not only to each other but to a way of life and to a role and place in community. They pledge themselves to reciprocal love and care (Eph. 5), to nonretaliation (Matt. 5), and to mutual correction and forgiveness (Matt. 18). They commit themselves to clarity (transparency) and faithfulness, where a simple "Yes" or "No" holds true (Matt. 5:37). The man and woman enter into the common way of the Christian life bound together with the intensity of their love and in a union that is for them a new path and promise of life.

It is a good sign, I think, when friends and family lavish the new couple with gifts. It is a sign that the new husband and wife are not, in fact, starting a new family. They are not going to carry on alone. In my younger days, I was critical of the number and kind of wedding gifts. I used to think that the profusion of dishes, pots, pans, tablecloths, gravy boats, candlesticks, bath towels, and bedspreads commercialized and diminished the occasion. In some cases, the excesses of gifts, tuxedos, and wedding receptions do, in fact, cheapen the day. However, I now realize that in many instances there is a different kind of economy at work. A community is investing in a home. A community is outfitting a home for key practices of sharing life, for hospitality, faithfulness, and longevity. A community offers gifts that are the nuts and bolts for a long and happy life of maintaining a household and raising children. So much can go wrong for a married couple, and it is a good sign when a community wants to help from the start.

This conception of marriage is familiar for Christians; nonetheless, for many of us, we find that there is a snag or hurdle that we have to struggle over once we are married. It is a hard reality for our culture that the customary practices of dating and courtship do not correspond to the habits and virtues of husbands and wives. When we date, we are face to face. You and I spend time alone with each other in order to discover how we are together. We go to movies and dinner by ourselves, and even when we attend gatherings, we travel, arrive, and depart on our own. We develop a romantic relationship, just you and I, and our best moments are free from intrusion, where we are able to look deeply into each other's eyes.

The romance of "you and I" brings us to the altar, but sooner or later we are cast out into the real world of home repair, electric bills, diapers, soccer practice, and work. It may take weeks, months, or a few years, but in time we will discover that we are seldom simply face to face. We live side by side. The image of our relationship is no longer the isolated pair in a restaurant as much as it is teammates on a field of play. We depend upon each other, but "the relationship" is no longer the focus of our lives. We attend to homework and childish skirmishes in the house, and to helping a spouse through a difficult time at work. With the long days (and sometimes long nights with sick children), there is added burden. We have pledged to share this life, for richer for poorer, in sickness and in health, till death do we part.

This added burden of the vow, I suspect, is the reason that "living together" has become prominent. In recent decades, sociologists have found, much to their surprise, that couples who marry after living together are more likely to divorce. The expectation had been the opposite. The earlier view was that a couple could have an informal trial marriage, and then if it seemed to be working out, they would move on to the formal and more permanent relationship. By and large, the motive for living together has turned out to be much different. Living together is attractive because, like dating, it is provisional and always open to negotiation. The couple is always able to reevaluate the relationship. In other words, the logic of dating is sustained insofar as the value of the relationship is judged on the "face to face" quality of the "you and I." This reasoning also explains why having children together does not keep these informal relationships together. A population study in the mid-1990s concluded that "the substitution of cohabitation for marriage is a story of lower commitment of women to men and even more so of men to women and to their relationship as an enduring unit." Men, in particular, want the companionship of living together (the romance) without the distractions and burdens of children and a home.

We live in a culture where marriage is a joke. It is not necessarily a cruel joke, but it is the stuff of situation comedy: the everyday misunderstandings among husband and wife, adolescent thoughtlessness and scheming, small crises that appear to be beyond repair, and finally resolution and reconciliation. There is some truth in viewing marriage as a comedy. When we take our vows, for richer and for poorer, we do so with a recklessness that we may or may not recognize. We are committing ourselves to a shared life without seeing the product—like buying a pig in a poke. We have good understanding of the character of our beloved, but we have little idea of the joys and sorrows that our lives together will bring. We have little idea of how we will deal with tragedies, extended periods of struggle, or a year or two of boredom. Marriage, in our time, is an adventure for foolish lovers. If a couple is interested in a cost-benefit analysis, they should probably just live together so that one or the other can back out when the monotony or tragedy hits.

Modern marriage is comic in some respects, but the picture given by the typical sitcom is ultimately tragic. In the typical television program, the foibles and misfortunes of marriage are resolved by a renewal of romantic appreciation. In other words, husband and wife are renewed by a face-to-face moment. They are able to turn away from the dishes and dirty laundry and focus on each other—on their relationship. The message here, I think, is that romance can overcome all troubles, and that youthful love can endure. This is the tragedy: marriage endures only if we never grow up, if our love never moves beyond the immaturity of dating. From the point of view of Christian love, it is indisputable that love will last, but the enduring love is not romantic. In this respect, the sitcom perpetuates a comic deception: for love to endure the foolish lovers must remain romantic fools. Christians, in contrast, are called to a higher love of friendship with God. We might be well aware that feelings of romance will get us into marriage, but they will not sustain us. Romantic love makes promises ("till death do we part") that it cannot keep.

Friendship sustains the promise, and this difference between romance and friendship is why marriage is superior to dating and living together. Romantically, we desire to give ourselves over to another. In friendship, we are called to live side by side, animated by a common vision and progressing toward a common goal. If romance draws individuals outside of themselves, friendship draws the pair outside of "the relationship." The friendship of God draws us to a love that we cannot sustain on our own in our private moments of loving face to face. We are called to join together to increase in faithfulness. The friendship of God draws us to a life where love is actually found (rather than undermined) in hard times and through the pedestrian activities of home. The wonder of grace is that it comes not only to the blessed or the misfortunate, but into the ordinary people who gather in God's name. The friendship of God has already drawn us into communion with the poor, lame, blind, imprisoned, sick, and our enemies. From this love, it is no great leap to pledge "for richer, for poorer, in sickness and in health."

9

Sex and Singleness

In the contrast between romance and friendship, marriage represents general tensions within our social relationships. The impermanence of romance, dating, and living together corresponds to much of what has been discussed in previous chapters about our cultural-economic logic of detachment and temporary usefulness. In a world dominated by the free market, the enduring love of marriage makes little sense. Our economy and our world of social detachment are a training ground where we are not likely to learn the skills required for lasting commitments. Marriage imposes requirements of endurance, patience, humility, and self-scrutiny that may be too great for most of us to bear. To this degree, our desire and struggles to learn how to honor our wedding vows are part of the work of living faithfully as a church. Marriage is not a unique case, but it is a clear case where various problems come into relief and where we can seek a deeper understanding of God's love for the world. Moving from this discussion of marriage and its contrast with romantic love, I will make similar connections and contrasts between love and sex, and then between love and the call of living a single life.

To introduce sex, I begin with the power of sexual desire. Desire generally, not merely sexual desire, is a yearning and a longing for movement toward union with someone or something. If I desire pie, the image of it will preoccupy and haunt my mind. If I want rest from this preoccupation, I will eat something else in hope that my desire will be diverted (at least for a time), or I will drive to a diner ten miles away. By the time I clink my fork on an empty plate (for the second or third time), I will be satisfied. Ironically, the more often that I am satisfied, my desire for pie will be more frequent and intense. My ten-mile drive may become a habit. However, I cannot escape the intensity of desire by simply avoiding pie altogether. I know that pie is out there, and the yearnings of hunger will strike me in any case. So, when I simply see those beautiful pies rotating under glass, and when the image is added to my preexisting hunger, pie begins to haunt my mind. I desire union.

Given the workings of desire, it is no surprise that sexual desire is used to draw us to products, people, places, and things. Few of us are tricked by the image of a woman in a bikini sitting on the hood of a sports car. Few men imagine that sexy women would fall all over us if we were to own a particular automobile. The message is more subtle. Before going further, I should mention that I recently watched a similar commercial advertising a pickup truck. The truck was backing a boat into a lake, and big-breasted women in bikinis were emerging from the cab of the truck. The women just kept coming, and if they had not been such a glorious sight, the viewers would have been reminded of the circus trick where an implausible number of clowns emerge from a tiny little car. Although implausible and ridiculous, the commercial works. The truck company has spent millions to produce it, and advertising companies know what they are doing. What is going on?

Truck buyers know that the commercial is silly and that the events pictured will never happen to them. But reality is not the point. Providing an entirely different reality is the aim of the advertisement. The point is that an "otherworldly" commercial can conjure up *desire* for an experience, rather than a guarantee for the experience itself. The point of a barrage of big-breasted women is not to suggest that the truck will be the means for sexual satisfaction. On the contrary, the commercial will be successful if it produces a sense of sexual dissatisfaction, which can be generalized and transferred. For the advertisement to work well, the women will be unattainable. They will represent a world entirely different from our own. If you have seen the commercial, you know that the bodies of these women are not within the reach of nature. Even their bodies are unattainable except as commercially enhanced. I dare say that such women will not be found in the truck buyer's house or neighborhood. The point of the advertisement is that the truck lifts us out of our ordinary lives into the desire-fulfillment of another world. If the truck commercial does its work, our way of looking at the everyday world will be changed. After enjoying an image of the "other" world, the brief commercial experience should stick in our minds so that we will be a little less satisfied with our own lives, with our old dirty trucks or mind-numbing minivans.

In short, sexual desire is an effective economic means to create feelings of dissatisfaction. It is not sexual fulfillment that drives us to want more, but anxiety about our lack of fulfillment—or lack of a "sexy" way of life. In the Greek world, men welcomed old age because, among other reasons, they would be free from the preoccupations of youthful desires. According to this logic, we are able to be satisfied more often and to a greater degree when our desires are not as persistent and intense. Our modern logic is the opposite. When desire starts to settle within us, we take Viagra. We worry that we might be too easily satisfied, that we have lost our drive. Wanting, desiring, and needing are as important as attaining what we desire and far more important than a sense of satisfaction. Sexual language and images are almost everywhere in our culture because they are effective means to produce and transfer more and more desire. Our growth economy functions well when we are able to generate more desire so that more and more goods and services need to be produced.

This "economy of desire" corresponds to widely accepted sexual habits and basic social attitudes concerning sex. By and large, sex is considered a fundamental form of self-expression, and our sexual self is considered most free and vital when we are single and only loosely committed in our sexual relationships. Marriage might be considered superior in interpersonal terms, but in matters of sexual fulfillment, the single life is believed to offer opportunity and access for a full expression of the sexual drive. With an economic analogy, we can say that marriage imposes a monopoly, and singleness sustains the variety, availability, and competitive prices of the free market. Marriage, in contrast, inflates the cost of sexual companionship, and therefore, couples are turning toward living together as a less binding option. Within this framework, however, love and sex are fundamentally at odds. On one hand, sex needs freedom. On the other, sexual love is an intense form of self-giving that seeks to monopolize the two selves. Fulfillment in love must be traded against the cost of sexual desire.

Some sociologists and theologians will argue that sex within marriage is actually more fulfilling. Some studies claim that couples who do not have sexual intercourse before marriage are on the whole more fulfilled in marriage. This may be true for some or many married couples, but in terms of Christian vows of marriage, the point is irrelevant. Marriage does not serve the purpose of sexual fulfillment, even though, in fact, it may be (or may not be) found in the steadfast fidelity of a couple's common life. The standard wedding vows do not include statements that refer to the quality of a sexual relationship. In the church, couples are expected to accept each other and to try their best to care for the other person in matters of sex. Mutual care is all that we can demand and expect. In 1 Corinthians 7, Paul teaches husbands and wives to give their bodies over to each other so that their desires will be put to rest as much as possible. Paul's thinking is that once our desires are settled we can put our minds to other more important things, namely to the coming kingdom of God.

Singleness, for Paul, represents an ideal, not for the sake of sexual opportunities, but because sex is excluded as a concern. This idea seems unreasonable to many of us. It reverses the way that Christians now typically think of singleness and marriage. Christians today tend to think that singleness ought to serve marriage. We ought to endure a sexless life of singleness in order to save ourselves for marriage. Marriage is the goal. Paul, on the other hand, assumes that marriage ought to look as much like singleness as possible. In 1 Corinthians 7, singleness is the goal. Singleness, for Paul, is an elevation of our natures that depends upon life within the family of God. Singleness is a sign. In our world, it can be a sign of loneliness and a lack of love. However, in the history of Christianity (until recently), singleness is a sign of the riches of common life. It is the opportunity to give ourselves more fully to others in love of God and neighbor. It is freedom, not for loose commitments and sexual opportunity, but for deeper bonds to people whom we can love and serve, such as our neighbors, brothers and sisters, the sick, the poor, and the imprisoned.

If singleness is a state of life in its own right, sex within marriage begins to look different. In our culture of sexual access, sex is a basic drive and image of vitality and the "fullness of life." In an economy driven by producing more desire, sexual desire corresponds to a need to desire more and more. Sex becomes an image of economic excess and loose attachments, which give opportunity for restlessness and freedom. Sexual desire requires a kind of nomadic existence, where desire pushes us to imagine having what we do not yet have and living in a world that is not yet our own. The Christian life represents an entirely different kind of homelessness, where we accept hospitality as a gift and settle into a place. Christian singleness and marriage alike form an alternative. In each, we are called to resist self-serving habits, to give ourselves over to the needs of others, and to be critical of our own desires. We are called, even in marriage, to submit sexual desire to our greater desire for friendship with God, spouse, and neighbor.

If sex is a representative image of cultural excess and detachment, then singleness within the church is the contrasting image. We should accept that it is a mark against our faithfulness when we lack the kind of communities that can sustain the single life as one that is rich in friendship, intimacy, purpose, and love. In sexual matters, as well as marriage and family, we have before us the adventure of community and the gift of God's hospitality. When we are open to God's bounty, we are not able to follow Jesus alone. We are brothers and sisters in Christ. We are brothers and sisters before we are married or single. Before we are husbands and wives, fathers and mothers, we are gathered as God's friends.

We have the shared task of seeking an alternative to the isolated home and privatized notions of love. As I have noted, the place of single people in our communities puts this alternative to the test. It is interesting that sexual desire and romantic love in our culture often follow the logic of contractual relationships. Certainly two people who fall in love want to give themselves to each other fully. They seek unconditional love. But popular conceptions of sex and romance have difficulty withstanding the pressures of day-to-day life at work and at home. The "face to face" of romance may not survive the "side by side" of common endeavors—of raising children, maintaining a home, and caring for neighbors. Ironically, when passion and romantic love die, a man and a woman who were once starry-eyed and love struck may find that they have no use for each other. This kind of disappointment and loss of passion reveals a hidden way that we use one another through romantic love. We use each other if our love has no purpose except our private bonds. The antidote to this abuse of love is the friendship of God.

Conclusion

■ This first part of the book began with the plenty of American culture and the restlessness of the out-of-control economy, and it has ended with the lonely and austere cultural image of the single, sexless life. In challenging popular conceptions of love and passion, I wanted to end with a clear sense of denial and resistance, of what we give up in leading the Christian life. In between American plenty and the austerity of Christian sexual ethics, in the heart of this part of the book, I have attempted to picture and to emphasize the greater bounty and hospitality of the friendship of God. I am suggesting that we Christians take up a kind of middle-class asceticism—a simplicity and moderation of life. I am suggesting that we live a different way in this world of desire-fulfillment and abundance in order to open ourselves to the bonds of common life, friendship, and the self-giving love of God. We begin by gathering as a people in worship and prayer, and we should expect that doing so will transform our relationship to the world. God's love gives us light to see our neighbors and to envision and desire a higher justice. We are called to order our lives according to God's mercy and grace.

The church is called to take up a special relationship to the world. I have encouraged a critical eye toward our everyday lives not for the purposes of cynicism, detachment, or contempt, but for a greater love and deeper relationships to God and our neighbors. Our lives are ordered by various roles and obligations to people, by "our place" in relation to our parents and children, employers and employees, teachers, students, neighbors, family, and friends. The fundamental role and purpose for the church, however, is to be people of peace—to be a people gathered in the friendship and hospitality of God. From this call to be a people, I now turn explicitly, in Part 2, to the question of "our place."

63

Part 2

Places

Introduction

■ Insofar as Part 1 dealt with themes of friendship and family, this second part of the book attends to how Christians are called to dwell in a place. The topic is how we settle in the world as our home. It is tempting, sometimes, to idealize the home as a place of harmony and good will. As a father, I know different. I like to tell my disbelieving college students that parenthood is about cleaning up excrement (the baby's, the cat's, the rabbit's, and the chicken's) and breaking up fights (with four children, there is a variety of one-on-one and two-on-one combinations). These two activities are constants, and how we are able to deal with them is a good measure of how we are getting along at home. As easy as it is to idealize a place, we can become cynical as well. In wanting a place to be better, we might be tempted to think that it is the worst place of all. It is not unusual to hear people attribute all the pain of their adult life to dysfunctions in their childhood homes. They view freedom from the corruption of home as their central purpose in life. We Christians are called to live between these two extremes, between idealizing our place in the world and taking flight from it. We are called to bring peace by following Jesus with faith and hope.

10

Our Place

■ John Lennon provided a generation with expressions of hope, love, and peace. "All you need is love" and "give peace a chance" may sound naïve, but when set against a world of hate and strife, the lyrics seem important. The simplicity of the songs is ingenious. In composing "All You Need Is Love," Lennon surely could have expanded on the theme, but he seems to have had the insight that he could not add any positive content to love, if all you need is love. "There's nothing you can do that can't be done. Nothing you can sing that can't be sung." The double negative is clever. It hides the hollowness of the message. If "all you need is love," that is all that needs to be said. "Nothing you can say but you can learn how to play the game. It's easy." There is nothing to add. "All you need is love."

I take Lennon to be a representative of his age. He is a typically modern romantic who seeks transcendence and liberation from all the social structures and systems that divide us and corrupt our natures. Underlining the sentiment "all you need is love" is a modern desire for detachment, away from our parochial and unsophisticated neighborhoods, ideals, and commitments. Lennon certainly sounds socialist at times, but good capitalists can sing along, and Lennon can make a little money on it too. Both socialists and capitalists share the modern conception of the independent inner self. For Lennon, the ideal is the lone individual, not in nature, but in the city and marketplace, where every individual is unique yet fundamentally the same, where differences are only a matter of style, and where style is embraced with indifference. Nothing goes deep, so "all you need is love."

Like love, "give peace a chance" appears to be apolitical. According to Lennon's lyrics, peace gives a preferred place to no one. Amid talk of various "isms," this-ism and that-ism, revolution, integration, United Nations, Timothy Leary, and Alan Ginsberg, "all we are saying is give peace a chance." Again, Lennon makes his point negatively. Peace requires a rejection of ideology and partisan claims about the world. Peace requires that the independent self wrestle free from points of view. Lennon's song "Imagine" makes this theme of detachment plain. We will find peace if only we can imagine no heaven, no hell, no countries, no religion, and no possessions. The unity of everyone in nothing in particular.

Because the overall point of "Imagine" is hopeful, the negativity and destructiveness of the song is easy to miss. Nonetheless, peace, in Lennon's view, requires that our lives be unearthed. All people must be disabused of attachments to things and places and to their own dreams of heaven and fears of hell. Peace will come when we have no particular place to be or to go, and no particular future to imagine as our own. Through negation, Lennon imagines unity. An Eastern philosophy of selflessness might be at work, except that Lennon's unity includes all people in this earthly life, not their release from it. There is universal brotherhood in his mind's eye. This unity, however, is a conception of the mind, not a community. Lennon's dream is abstract. If we have no particular attachments and hopes, who are we? Who are all the people of Lennon's imagination? Where do we look? I suspect that we are to look at ourselves and imagine that a nonspecific human being is underneath what we have, who we love, and where we dwell. We become family through a kind of anonymity. It is difficult to grasp this nonspecific mental picture of "all the people." I really cannot imagine it.

This image of the modern utopia is worlds apart from the homelessness of Jesus. "Foxes have holes, and birds of the air have nests; but the Son of Man has nowhere to lay his head" (Matt. 8:20). Jesus' itinerancy in the world is God's way of taking our place and gathering the tax collector and the fisher, the Pharisee and the sinner, the lame and the blind. It is a scandal really, "foolishness" to the Greeks, that God would be so attached to creation and become human in a specific place and time. Jesus takes a specific place in relation to the world and asks us to follow. Unlike Lennon's "Imagine," this place is particular and imaginable as a way in the world today. With the church, we are already on a journey, and the people are called to gather in God's light now. The Pharisee, the tax collector, and fisher are called to take a specific role and place in relation to God and the world. "You are the salt of the earth" (Matt. 5:13). "You are the light of the world. . . . let your light shine before others, so that they may see your good works and give glory to your Father in heaven" (Matt. 5:14–16).

It is imaginable that these people can set out upon a way of reconciliation and light, whatever their number and however motley and unqualified they are for the role. It is imaginable that this people will not allow violence and resentment to be the final word. Their way of living and following the itinerant Jesus is not a route to rejection and flight, but a way of being at home. They will leave their gifts before the altar and go out in order to seek reconciliation with their brothers and sisters (Matt. 5:21–26). It is imaginable that they will work to train their eyes to see others without lust and envy. It is imaginable that they will stay by each other in sickness and in health, in times of plenty and in times when they are lacking. It is imaginable that their words will hold good; that their "Yes" will be "Yes" and their "No" will be "No" (Matt. 5:37). It is imaginable that talking about love and peace are just the beginning—that they have a long way to go.

It is imaginable that they will not seek revenge and retaliation. They will respond neither by striking back nor by passively suffering coercion and threats of force. It is imaginable that this people will act and seize the opportunity to give their coats when their shirts are taken away, and to carry a load two miles when pressed into service for one. They will not have to be coerced. They will serve. It is imaginable that they will hope and pray for their enemies and seek their good. It is imaginable that they will resist an ever-present temptation of evil, which is to live as though God is not the beginning and end of all. They will be tempted to live as though evil is an effective means to an end, and to live as though violence and enmity, war and subterfuge are means to do good. It is imaginable that this people will seek to be children of God, who "makes his sun rise on the evil and on the good, and sends rain on the righteous and on the unrighteous" (Matt. 5:45).

The way of being salt and light is a role (a part and position) that Christians are called to in the world. It is a role that requires us to take up a place in our world, at work, at school, and in the neighborhood. Christians are called to imagine another world, and to do so by living amid the divisiveness, alienation, suffering, and violence, as well as the good things, the loves and hopes of where we live now. It is imaginable that these Christian people will fail to live as they are called. Ironically, it is part of their role to recognize and to name their faults and their hypocrisy. We will represent the divisions and alienation of the world. However, we are called to make a home that is not established on our own authority and perfection, but instead is set on the foundation of repentance, forgiveness, mutual care and correction, and reconciliation.

A few years ago, I entered upon a semester-long argument with students based on the story of a young man named Chris McCandless. McCandless was a serious, hard working, and strong-willed college student. He did well in his classes and in sports, but he wanted more out of life. He felt despair over the superficiality, greed, and selfishness of the world. He wanted more. While in college, he began to take wilderness adventures, and after college he gave away all that he owned (including $25,000 in savings), and he set out on a quest. He drove across the country, and when his car broke down, he left it. He left his identity behind as well. He virtually cut off contact with his family, and he befriended strangers using the name "Alex." No one knew who he was. He was attached to nothing. He took up odd jobs, and, when necessary, he lived on the streets. Eventually, he set out into the wilderness of Alaska, and he died there, alone.

The students in my class where fascinated with McCandless's story. A few students had introduced the story of his life to the class; we read a few articles about him, and he dominated the rest of the semester. The students believed that McCandless was an example to be followed, at least in the spirit of his quest. He was able to find himself through his journey into the unknown, independent and alone in the world. I thought otherwise, and we had one of those conversations between a parent/teacher and young adults that is never resolved.

My side: How could McCandless "find" himself if he avoided being himself? He lived anonymously, under the alias "Alex." How could he find himself in flight from the world? What and who would he "be" when he returned?

The students' response: That is exactly how he must find himself. He must separate himself and go into the wilderness in order to find out who he truly is.

My counter: The wilderness is a time-honored place for a quest, but monks and mystics were not looking for themselves, but for God and the depth of God's relationship to the world. For this reason the "wilderness," in the Christian tradition, becomes not a place of flight but of pilgrimage and gathering. The recluse, strangely enough, was usually an active member of a desert community. Women and men in the desert drew a crowd.

The students' rebuttal: In order to find himself, McCandless has to separate himself. He must set out alone to find himself alone.

This conversation put in clear relief the contrast between modern romantic flight and ancient practices of "otherworldliness." Chris McCandless was a good-hearted young man who felt the weight of the world upon him. He was ambitious and talented, but youthful. For a parent, his story does not provide an example as much as an occasion for sadness. His life and death bring the modern search for the lone self to its obvious conclusion. He dies anonymously and alone. In contrast, if we are looking for God and looking forward to God's friendship, we are called to take our place and role among others. Whether we forge out into the desert or accept the hospitality of strangers, we set up a home.

11

The Home and the Hospitality of the Market

■ For many of us, the home is no longer a place to spend time, but a dwelling where we sleep, sometimes eat, and usually spend our weekends. We Americans spend a lot of time on the road, making contact with our loved ones via cell phones and e-mail. I have heard some people refer to their cars as their homes. Alternatively, an increasing number of people are working at home, using Internet communication and fax machines in order to play their part in a business or to make a business of their own. New forms of technology have given us instant access to each other and have allowed us to fit a great deal of activity into an ordinary day. By and large, this access, immediacy, and efficiency have brought more work. Work draws us out of the home, and work might draw us back. In each case, the home serves work. In the way that we tend to go about our business, there is no good in just being in a place, in cultivating a home for inviting people in, and living side by side.

There is a rising desire to slow down and to simplify life. A recent *Parade* magazine featured advice for those of us who feel that they have lost control of our lives (August 5, 2001). "You *Can* Find the Time" offers suggestions for escaping from the rush of the upwardly mobile. It offers an antidote to the feeling that we are working to make our lives better and in the process missing life. The article tells the story of Richard

Erickson and his wife Mary Harding. Years ago, they would rise at 5:00 A.M., drop their child off at daycare, and commute in opposite directions to demanding but promising jobs. When they came home, they brought their work with them. If time remained, they cleaned and got the house in order. Erickson remembers that he "felt a nagging emptiness. The way we were living had to change."

"You *Can* Find the Time" offers a plan to "gain control of your life." The following is the article's inventory:

- List your most deeply felt priorities and goals. Take some quiet time and ask yourself if the way you spend your time matches the list.
- Keep a log of your spending to identify ways to reduce financial pressure.
- Set aside time each day to reflect on what is important.
- Explore flextime or work-at-home options to reduce stress on the job.
- Restrict TV viewing to shows that you value. [The article also notes that "the average American adult spends up to 25 hours a week in front of the tube."]
- Turn off your cell phone, pager, and fax at the end of the workday.
- Limit your Internet use to the purposes you really care about.
- Develop relationships by allowing yourself time for conversation, letter-writing, and shared activities.
- Analyze your schedule to see where it might be simplified by reducing commuting time, errands, and chores.
- Sell or give away possessions you haven't used for six months.
- Allow your children only one extracurricular activity at a time.

The list tells us some interesting things about our lives. First, so-called "time-saving" technology is not saving but is dominating our time. Second, we are acquiring many things that offer distractions, but these things do not improve the quality of our lives. For instance, because television can quickly become uninteresting, many of us seek relief from this boredom by acquiring cable service or a satellite dish (each with the promise of more channels) and a big-screen TV. The assumption is that the quantity of channels and the size of the picture will improve the medium. More of the same kind of programming might be interesting for awhile, but in the end the quality of our lives will have stayed the same.

Third, note that the article's route to happiness is dependent upon "taking control of our lives." At this point, I will begin to criticize the article for supporting the problems that it intends to solve. Its diagnosis

73

of the problem is a good start, but the advice of "You *Can* Find the Time" does not go far enough. In the article, simplifying one's life is conceived as a privilege of those who can choose from a variety of careers and easily shift from one good job to another. Next, the piece in *Parade* suggests that many of us do not think about life in terms of purpose. The first item on the list counsels us to take an inventory of our priorities and goals, but it does not introduce the idea that our lives might have a purpose beyond our private interests and attitudes about our happiness. "Taking control of our lives" is conceived as a turn inward. Finally, the home is assumed to be a refuge or retreat from the world, unless one sets up an office there. The home is inwardly directed, a place where we think through our private priorities and goals.

In the chapter on family in Part 1, I appealed to an ancient understanding of the church as our first family. Likewise, if we Christians call the church our first home, then the home is not so much a private retreat or haven but a place of gathering and generosity, a place where we are called to live into and live out the hospitality of God. *Parade* offers a list of great suggestions for removing the excess clutter from our lives, and we ought to take this turn toward simplicity to heart. However, I would like to suggest that our American problems of excess and overload apply not only to time but to place. This is where the article is lacking. If "time-savers" are dominating our time, and if increased productivity and efficiency are leaving us empty, the refuge of home might be isolating us; in the pursuit of private happiness, we might find ourselves all alone.

Parade's "You *Can* Find the Time" implies that the American penchant for work, productivity, and upward mobility is the root of the problem. Ironically, achievement and a pursuit of the good life take control of us, and we lose precious time to enjoy the good things in life. Granted, time is a problem, but there is also an issue of having or not having a place where we are deeply connected to others.

Many of us are tethered to our cell phones, pagers, and fax machines because we always want to be connected. I might admit that it is true that my time is dominated by work, but I will live with inconvenient calls, the pager, and the fax machine because work gives me a sense of purpose. At work, I take a valuable place in relation to others. I might admit that it is true that I am held down by debt and by all the things that I have acquired, but in our world, the marketplace is the arena of social life. The private home is no competitor to the market. By shopping, I enter the equivalent of the town commons, and by buying, owning, and consuming new things, I sustain an active role and rightful place. I fashion my identity in relation to others as we share a vision of the good life. From the market, I fashion my home.

Our shopping malls are spacious, safe from the heat and the cold, full of colorful and interesting things, and well populated with regular folk, not in a rush but leisurely enjoying the place. Going to the mall is something to do in itself, whether one is young or old. In the least, it is a way to get out of the house. At best, it is a way to enjoy walking about, eating, and looking around amid the low hum of talk and activity. We can enjoy life upon a landscape that corporations and their employees have spent great amounts of money and effort to make appealing and inviting. A mall in suburban Baltimore advertises that its real product is not clothes or shoes, but a revitalizing experience. Arundel Mills boasts that the mall's "shoppertainment" will transform your life.

After her retirement and while still active, my mother befriended a group of sociable and like-minded men and women over coffee at McDonalds. For a good stretch, she headed to McDonalds almost every morning of the week. I have spent time at McDonalds myself, especially when we were enduring the winters of upstate New York—it provided a Saturday morning of coffee, a biscuit, the newspaper, and, most importantly, an indoor playland for the children. I never encouraged anyone to leave. I would act out a script that could have been a commercial. The kids are ready to go, but Dad wants to stay. McDonalds was my refuge.

"Every form of refuge has its price" (to cite the Eagles). Since our Saturday mornings at McDonalds, we have learned to call the Happy Meal the "Disappointing Meal," because it doesn't seem to make anyone happy, and it certainly is not a meal. Food is only a small part of the McDonalds experience, but still, we would return home grumpy. It seems that most of the company's TV ads appeal to relationships as the product. The product is partly the smiling employees, special moments with our children, children enjoying friendship and magic with Ronald McDonald, and a connection with the world of a Disney movie. Happy Meals are all about the toys, and most of the toys are about the wonderful world of Disney. Our trips to McDonalds were an escape and distraction from home. The distraction would last about thirty minutes, but the price of escape was that we were not learning the habits of living well at home.

Amid the frustrations of home, it is easy to fall into the need for "controlled environments" and friendly places. For example, like McDonalds, Wal-Mart is not so much a store but a place and a world of possibilities. Greeters welcome visitors at the front door, and Wal-Mart advertisements emphasize personal relationships. Customers feel at home, and families and friends happily shop together. Wal-Mart stores are town squares for the young and old, cheerleaders, senior citizen groups, and clowns. According to their advertisements, Wal-Mart employees do not just work at the store. The "associates" form a community. They are energized by teamwork. They volunteer together in community service, and they are

Wal-Mart's best customers. They love their stores. They come together with the customers for the most inviting aspect of Wal-Mart: a wide selection and low prices.

Are you skeptical? Well, it's all true, or at least it could be true. Wal-Mart is a great equalizer: hosts of people of various creeds, colors, and incomes all flock to their stores. Granted, it is a strange kind of hospitality. As my wife says about being treated like family at the Olive Garden restaurant, the next time her in-laws come to visit, she is going to draw up a bill. Likewise, I meet the Wal-Mart greeters with a cynical hello. But if there is a place of gathering in our society, the superstore or shopping mall is it.

Perhaps, like me, you are terribly out of fashion and enter a mall or Wal-Mart only when coerced. You may be ensconced at home or busy at work. You may have the kind of work that enriches your life. Unlike Richard Erickson, you may feel no nagging emptiness. Or like Erickson, you may have turned to private matters of home. However, it is undeniable that our places of consumption and commerce offer basic social settings in our cities and suburbs and that they provide fundamental forms of interpersonal exchange. Look around. You will see the Nike Swoosh, Adidas stripes, the Pepsi symbol, Tommy Hilfiger colors, cell phones, big screen televisions, PDAs, the letters of the Gap, Old Navy, and Abercrombie and Fitch. All these are the symbols, words, and hieroglyphics of our culture's wide-reaching and elastic social communication.

We are not "controlled" by products and advertisements, but they constitute a world of options and opportunities of expression. We wear Tommy Hilfiger or Dockers as individuals; personal choices are made. But if you do not want to display any product symbols, letters, or colors, you will have to be vigilant. They are part of the common language of our culture, and they may soon be upon you. The trouble is not that we are mindlessly controlled by things; instead, a marketplace of things provides our most pervasive common language, and this shared language shapes a common world. Many of us are dominated by things (hurried by "time savers" and burdened by luxury items), but we think of these things as solutions, perhaps because we do not seem to have any place else to go.

12

Sharing, Eating,
and Housekeeping

■ Certainly, there is more to common life than malls, department stores, and Old Navy sweatshirts. People gather, spend time, and work together in a variety of ways and for a variety of reasons. Although we might find ways to resist, the market is a dominant organizational setting of our time, and consumption is a basic mode of entering this common space. Little league baseball players run out on the field with "Jiffy Lube" emblazoned on their backs, and just about everyone else is advertising something. Even political alternatives, religious values, and anticonsumerist messages appear on bumper stickers, billboards, and T-shirts. A person can paste a "Live Simply" bumper sticker on his or her Volvo so that others can see the message during the person's forty-mile commute to work.

As I write, I imagine that many readers are unconvinced. Many are satisfied that they are able to disengage themselves from the mainstream of social and economic life. Many of us believe that we can stand apart from the rest. I dare say, however, that this "standing alone" is precisely the problem. The market functions with a logic of individual detachment. If you are proud of your disengagement from the crowd, you may be most deeply imbued with the ideals of the market. The market offers nothing if not personal choice. It offers opportunity to stand alone. When all is said and done, some of us may be deceived in our confidence that we are not affected by market rationality, and some of us may not. Our lives may have already been colonized by the market, or we may be holed up in retreat. In either case, the issue is the manner by which we are bound to each other in a place. Again, the issue is not a matter of being controlled. The issue is how we are connected to a place and joined through a common language and vision of life.

Here, I will shift from the issue of place to the languages of our common life, which connect us in a place. For the church, the story of Pentecost provides a central image. "When the day of Pentecost had come, they were all together in one place" (Acts 2:1). The Spirit is given. The Spirit descends like a fierce wind, divides as in tongues of fire, rests on each person, and fills all who are gathered. Each person begins to speak in a different language. This foreign speech is not like the "tongues" that are known later among the Corinthian church. These "tongues," although heavenly, were unintelligible. In a letter to the Corinthians, Paul points out the limitations of such utterances. "I will be a foreigner to the speaker and the speaker a foreigner to me" (1 Cor. 14:11). By contrast, the day of Pentecost transcends the limitations of diverse languages. A crowd is gathered, and all are amazed "because each one heard them speaking in the native language of each. . . . Parthians, Medes, Elamites, and residents of Mesopotamia, Judea and Cappadocia, Pontus and Asia, Phrygia and Pamphylia, Egypt and the parts of Libya belonging to Cyrene, and visitors from Rome, both Jews and proselytes, Cretans and Arabs—in our own languages we hear them speaking about God's deeds of power" (Acts 2:6, 9–11).

The many languages of Pentecost reverse the dispersal of peoples in the story of Babel (Gen. 11:1–9). As the story of Babel begins, all the people of the earth have one language. They all gather in one place and begin to conspire to build a great city and a tower to the heavens and to make a name for themselves. The Lord sees their unity of mind and knows that "nothing that they propose to do will now be impossible for them" (11:6). In reaction, God scatters the people and confuses their languages. The Lord seems to be apprehensive about human ambitions, and, by confusion, God puts the competition to rest.

The picture of God is entirely different in Acts 2. God offers unity in human community. The Spirit descends at Pentecost and is given as God's new possibility for us to gather in one place. In Acts, the Spirit draws the attention of Jews, who have gathered in Jerusalem but come from the many nations of the diaspora. The people are gathered before Peter as they had been before Moses at Sinai and Joshua at Shechem. The story of God's salvation is remembered and told. Peter tells of God's wondrous works on behalf of Israel. He tells of God's plan of salvation in Jesus Christ, who was crucified and raised. Peter concludes his speech,

"For the promise is for you, for your children, and for all who are far away, everyone whom the Lord our God calls to him" (Acts 2:39).

The church is the place for the pilgrimage of all nations, even Gentile peoples. Through the Spirit, the church is constituted by people who are extended through the nations. The church is gathered and spread out from household to household by a common confession of faith, prayer, sharing the table, and breaking bread.

In Acts, the gathering of the Gentiles comes as a revelation and shock to Peter. While in the city of Joppa, Peter receives a vision of unclean creatures laid before him, reptiles, birds, and all kinds of four-legged creatures. In the vision, he is instructed to kill them and to eat. He resists, but he is commanded, "What God has made clean, you must not call profane" (Acts 10:15). Immediately afterward, Peter is escorted to the home of Cornelius, and he witnesses the Spirit's descent upon this Gentile's household. These Gentiles receive baptism in Christ's name. They believe. When Peter returns from Joppa, he has a good bit of explaining to do. His countrymen receive word that he has been entertained in a Gentile household and has eaten with them. He explains that, "the Holy Spirit fell upon them just as it had upon us at the beginning. . . . [And] who was I that I could hinder God?" (Acts 11:15–17).

What kind of place is the church—this house of gathering and breaking bread? I have a friend who says that the guitar is a superior instrument for Christian worship because bulky instruments like the organ and piano are not portable enough for a pilgrim people. I used the same line on our pastor when the folding chairs in our fellowship hall where replaced with heavier (but still stackable) upholstered chairs. Shouldn't we avoid being weighed down with stuff, financially and otherwise? Shouldn't we be heading outward rather than attending to comforts at home? Shouldn't we avoid thinking about the church as a building and as a distinct place?

I admit that I am one of those parishioners who moans every time money is spent on the physical structure or furnishings for the sanctuary or fellowship hall. I should add that I also grumble or silently resist every time money is spent on "nonessential" furnishings at home. I also admit that I am wrong. I am still the teenager who scoffs when my mother protects the "sanctity" of our living room from my brother and me for the benefit of the stranger and guest. I am still the young man who enjoys the appealing places of commerce but criticizes churches for their attractive buildings and meeting places. I am still the person who will look up in amazement at the Sears Tower, the Empire State Building, and even the relatively modest Corning Towers in Albany, New York. Every city has its high point. I have enjoyed splendid views from many cities, looking at the far horizon and the little things below. I have accepted the odd but common view that church steeples ought not to rival these buildings, but should be, from the highest vantage point, one of the many small spots near the ground.

It is true that the church should be among the low places. However, my uncritical admiration for the Sears Tower reveals a problem in my thinking about the church as a place. Even if I accept that the church is my first home, my conception of home has been a private conception, as a retreat and refuge apart from the world. My mother's conception of home corresponds to the right view of the church. When my mother would not allow me to use (or abuse) the best places in our house, I complained because I assumed that our home was only a space for our entertainment and comfort. What I realize now is that a house without guests is nearly empty, and the same holds for the church. My mother's understanding of our home had been shaped by God's hospitality, by Jesus' gathering of the lost. I realize now that my mother thought of herself as a guest, and like the guest at a great wedding feast, her sense of gratitude and appreciation incited a desire to share her bounty.

Dorothy Day, who lived and worked with the homeless of New York City, suggested that working- and middle-class families could invite Christ into their lives by setting aside a guest room in their homes, a Christ room, where the hungry and thirsty, homeless and sick could find shelter and care. If we were to put this idea in practice, we might need a relatively large and inviting household, with lots of comfortable chairs and warm beds. We may have to build a big house to be among the low places. This is the place of the church.

Because the church is our first home, our sanctuaries and fellowship halls should have plenty of space for us and other guests. The logic of our world is much different. When we drive by sprawling shopping malls, many of us see progress and opportunity. We drive by stately houses with spacious yards in newly fashioned neighborhoods, and we see the good life and the fruits of hard work and success. We drive by a grand church, and many of us see self-satisfaction and arrogance. Why do we look at tall churches in this way? It could be that a particular church, as "a city set on a hill," is like the large home in the exclusive neighborhood. It could be that the church building has become a private place. Many make this assumption, whether it is true for a particular congregation or not. Why? Could our way of seeing these places be all wrong?

It could be that we have accepted the common view that "religion" is a private matter, and like the suburban home, the church has no other purpose than for private use. Large homes in exclusive neighborhoods are acceptable because they are a matter of personal success and choice. Shopping malls are a private venture, an investment, and a common arena of commerce and opportunity. If religion is private, however, a splendid house of worship appears to be an attempt to take private possession of God, an attempt to take comfort in the accoutrements of a country club membership where one can rub shoulders with the divine. According to this logic (of the imperial economy), public places and the spaces of common life are made through contractual exchange, trade, and consumption. According to this logic, the large church looks like a religious shopping mall that is built to attract, impress, and provide privileged access to God.

This logic is all wrong of course, but I assure you that I am not making it up. While teaching confirmation classes at my church, I have heard these views expressed often by our teenagers who have been thoroughly formed within the religious and economic ways of our culture. I have heard these criticisms of the church from college teachers, business owners, mall-goers, and residents of stately houses in newly fashioned neighborhoods. It is almost beyond the common imagination of our time that when Peter proclaims Christ crucified and risen, and when many are baptized on the day of Pentecost, their immediate and natural response is to share their possessions, to spend a great deal of time together, and to break bread from household to household (Acts 2:40–47). To share and to eat is a different kind of economic bond.

Acts 5:1–6 records the disturbing story of Ananias and Sapphira. This husband and wife sell a bit of their land in order to contribute to common goods for common needs in the burgeoning Christian community. When Ananias brings the profit from the land to Peter, he does not give all the money that he had earned. Peter is perplexed not because Ananias and Sapphira have sold only a piece of land, but because they have sold some for the purpose of giving to the church, and then they have secretly held some of it back. Why lie? "While it remained unsold, did it not remain your own? And after it was sold, were not the proceeds at your disposal? How is it that you have contrived this deed in your heart? You did not lie to us but to God!" (Acts 5:4). Once accused, first Ananias and then later Sapphira drop dead. This kind of story makes people worry about the church's ambitions concerning property. But such an interpretation misses the issue: the problem is not what Ananias and Sapphira keep, but what they give with duplicity and half-hearted generosity. In reluctant and deceptive sharing in common life, there is death, but in giving truthfully, there is life.

A good measure of a place—of its generosity or reluctance to share in common life—is the food. It is a sign of a troubled home when there is no food in the cabinets and refrigerator. The trouble may be financial, or it may be neglect. It may be that no one spends time at home. It is a mark against hospitality when the cabinets are full but there is no food to serve to uninvited guests. It is a sign of a closed home when hospitality is occasional, when meals must be scheduled and highlighted as special events. The upwardly mobile family cannot afford to spend time in a hospitable home. Its members eat quickly because there is usually some place else to go. A hospitable home, in contrast, requires that the doors can be opened, that people are going about their business inside, and that the "business" is enlarged rather than interrupted by the guests. The meal is ready. The members of a hospitable home greet guests without looking back at the TV, fax machine, or computer. They greet uninvited guests as though, with their arrival, the day has now begun. It is the guests who are the measure of a home. When guests are fully welcome, they share the home. They clean up the dishes and answer the door. Such unreserved hospitality and "feeling at home" are rare indeed, because this kind of place requires the good work, the investment of time and resources, of keeping up a home.

The church is the household where we gather with people—some like us, some not, some who offer us assistance and advantages, and some who do not. In the church we are all guests who share, eat, and are acquainted with each other (befriended) through the sign of God's peace. For us Christians, the church is our first home. We are guests who reside, take part in food preparation, and open the door when someone knocks. As followers of Jesus, we are called to be bound to this kind of place. We are called to be good housekeepers, to have our cabinets full and food ready to serve. We are called to have plenty of empty chairs, attractive and comfortable, waiting to be filled. We are called to gather and to go about the kind of business that is enriched by the uninvited guest. To do so requires that we maintain an attractive place that gives honor to the guests.

"The church is not the building but the people." This popular saying is only half right. The church is the people, but the building—the place where they gather and share common life—is an important measure of the people. The church is not called to mimic glass skyscrapers by building crystal cathedrals. We are not called to tower over others, but we are called to elevate the low places. In drawing near to people, we take up space. We need to invest in it and to maintain it, to keep a hospitable home. We are called to share our resources, to give to the needy, and to cast off the folding chairs. They indicate that we do not expect anyone to be comfortable or to stay very long. It is a measure of the church that we care for the church building as our first and most hospitable and appealing home. There is more to common life than shopping malls, department stores, the Washington Monument, and the Sears Tower. The place is the church. It is where the low places are lifted up, and we have the opportunity to exchange a piece of land for sharing in life.

82

13

Country and Nation

■ The land is a bond. On various occasions when "America the Beautiful" is considered a suitable Sunday hymn, it is sung across the land with great feeling and respect. Most of us raised in the church can recite the first verse from memory. "O beautiful for spacious skies, for amber waves of grain, for purple mountains' majesties above the fruited plain." Singing this hymn expresses two aspects of the way that Christians dwell in a place: one hopeful and one hazardous. One side is our hope that our affections for the land and our fellow citizens will be harmonized by the love of God. The hymn expresses the point this way: "crown thy good in brotherhood," and "God mend thine every flaw, confirm thy soul in self control, thy liberty in law." In God, our loves and loyalties are not splintered and divided.

On this promising side, "America the Beautiful" articulates an expectation of unity, a firm belief that all of our loves will not be set against each other when ordered by the blessings and love of God. In God, we hope to find harmony among our love of the land and its people, as well as our love of righteousness and our love for all the peoples of the world. Boy Scouts dedicate themselves to both God and country. Presidents publicly bow their heads in prayer. At Mother Seton School, our children begin each day by reciting the Pledge of Allegiance, singing "My Country Tis of Thee," praying together, and then singing a hymn of thanksgiving and praise to God. We know that we cannot be loyal to a nation if this unity is not held together, and we sing with passion and ardently hope that being American is, in fact, good for the world. I think that this hope and passion reveal the depth of our call to love the world and to be bound to it as we follow in the way of Christ.

However, this love of our country and its inhabitants has a hazardous side. Love of country usually corresponds to an allegiance to a government, its history, and its power. This allegiance is a dangerous temptation. In biblical times and today, "the nations" are a chief rival to our faithfulness and dependence upon God. The temptation of "the nations" is upon us when we glorify a country and the ideals represented by a form of secular government. For Americans, the temptations are (1) to ally God's work with the successes and progress of our economy, (2) to assume that our military supremacy is part of God's plan, and (3) to see God's will for the world working through American democracy.

These three temptations of "the nations" have great power, so that this chapter is by far the most difficult and demanding in the book for me to write. I have put myself to self-scrutiny in writing it, and the reader may feel scrutinized as well. We receive and hope for great things from our nation, but we must have the courage to put our allegiance in its proper place. I will have cheated the reader if I do not indicate that faith in our economic and military power will draw us away from faith in God, even though the likely result is that the reader will only be embittered with me.

As I write (in March 2003), the U.S. has attacked Iraq, and our soldiers are fighting on the outskirts of Baghdad. Recently I heard a World War II veteran interviewed on the radio. When asked if the war in Iraq was just, he refused to answer. Instead, he said that the president has committed our troops to war, and that once we are committed, we ought not to question the president. Although it seems patriotic and noble, this kind of allegiance is precisely the view that Christians should guard against. In this view, those who wage war are given the benefit of the doubt. Implied in this view is an allegiance to a nation at war that trumps further considerations of faith.

When a nation goes to war, it is usually those who say "No" who must explain and justify their actions. The Christian faith reverses this imperative. The imperative of our faith is peace, and in time of war the benefit of the doubt goes to the peacemakers. If, after reading this chapter, you find its assertions unacceptable, I ask you to grant at least this point: from the point of view of the Christian faith, it is those who *do not* cry out against war who must justify their actions. Those Christians who see war as a great good have some explaining to do.

Blind faith in war begins early in life. Through years of civics and history lessons in elementary and high school, I learned that the history of civilization, from the Greek city-state until now, leads up to the United States. Because I learned to see America as the summit of history, I never learned to imagine a future for the world without American power and leadership. I do not think that these lessons were unusual or particular to an American school. Any nation or kingdom, if wise, trains its citizens to see the world and all of history through the lens of its own history and hopes. When young, I learned as my children now do about George Washington's presidency and Abe Lincoln's hard work and honesty. When older, I learned about the great wars of the twentieth century and America's key role in each.

The lessons were not harmful, but in the process I learned a lack of imagination. It is this lack of imagination that leaves us open to the temptations of "the nations." When I learned the history of American wars, I learned indirectly that there is no history after America and that military power makes a people great. I did not learn that in God's time all nations will rise and fall. I did not learn that the measure of a people is forgiveness and reconciliation. I did not learn that in God's time the sword will be melded to the plow. I did not learn to imagine such things, and this lack of imagination is at the heart of idolatry.

Faith in a nation tempts us to secure the future and our own good through military and economic strength, and to attach God's providence to the achievements of a worldly power. For the United States, the cost of military strength is over $1 billion each day. The proposed defense budget for 2004 is $379.9 billion. This figure is troubling. Although the U.S. seeks to promote democracy in the world, our worldwide military presence and threats of force are how we secure our position in the world. Our dependence on a military threat reveals a lack of imagination. This lack of imagination and its practical effects (on those in power as well as the weak) were denounced again and again by the prophets of Israel. Jeremiah cried out, "Do not learn the way of the nations" (Jer. 10:2).

It is interesting in this regard that Christians in America have been some of the most loyal soldiers *and* the most passionate war resisters. We have been the most dedicated patriots, and we have been the most critical opponents of the federal government, military power, and the economy of the "industrial-military complex." I suspect that these opposing passions, in the Christian life, have the same source. They emerge, I think, from our deep faith that the world is good, that we are called to order all things to God, and that we have a special role and responsibility to live for God—to be signs of God's reign of righteousness and peace.

To this degree no one is able to argue on Christian grounds that military force is an acceptable means to take possession of the land or to secure economic superiority over another people. Can we usher in the good of life through military conquest? Should a church in a troubled area of the globe hire mercenaries to protect its missionaries? Should the gospel be spread by the sword? Should we witness to our faith with a hand on a trigger? Along the same line of inquiry, there have been long debates in Christianity about if and how we might be soldiers. Medieval crusaders, who went to war in order to take hold of the Holy Land, serve as a reminder that the best intentions can be wrong. In response to the history of the Crusades, most agree that Christians cannot kill for Christ. Further, it is claimed that Christian soldiers are called to die rather than fight for unjust and self-serving purposes. They are called to die rather than kill or coerce in ways that are excessive or harmful to innocent people, whether compatriot or foreign, allied or enemy populations. Those who defend just wars propose on Christian grounds that we resist the temptation to use war simply as a means to advance personal self-interest or the ways and power of a nation.

Glorifying our own nation is a great temptation. The glory of the nation makes room for a new kind of crusade, where we kill for our country even though we would not kill for Christ. The new kind of crusade puts war at the service of our righteousness. If we can give our own nation glory far beyond our adversaries or allies, then our misdeeds and self-interest in the use of force will pale in comparison to our good. If we are better than the rest, then we can say that weapons are safe in our hands. If we are better than other nations, then we have a moral responsibility to keep weapons safe in our own hands. We will feel the responsibility to crusade for justice. With the glory of the nation behind us, we will feel called to save others through war and to crusade for democracy and peace. Glorifying our country makes us susceptible to false pride and prone to the view that our interests in war are entirely good.

In the tradition of Christian thought on war, the just warrior must reject these self-aggrandizing motives. For those who accept the possibility of war, this possibility is thought to be both rare and grim. Soldiers risk their lives for the sake of innocent people, not to stabilize the world oil market, not to topple governments, and not to take possession of the land. Likewise, Christian pacifists do not consider issues and problems of war in terms of their own preservation and self-interest. Christians who resist the use of military force do so because they would rather die than hold up the ways and power of a nation through killing. They would rather undermine their own interests than turn to war. They often accept imprisonment, derision, and destitution as the result of living in peace. Christian pacifism is a witness of courage and hope.

War resisters, however, have their own temptations—not to glorify a nation, but to look upon fellow citizens with cynicism and contempt. There are, in the U.S., significant numbers of people who are critical of our nation's use of power, but are as quick as the most ardent nationalist to divide people, nations, and history into the evil and the good. They consider the U.S. government and its people the leading source of economic and political corruption in the world. Here, the cynic's own country is considered not the summit of goodness, but the lowest of all. Cynics usually withdraw into a disdainful arrogance. They live without hope. Along these lines, secular war resisters in recent times have been tempted by their contempt and have turned to street violence while proclaiming the cause of peace. They have become like those they disdain.

In short, the two main temptations of "the nations" are glorifying one's government and people or showing contempt. It is not surprising, therefore, that these two options were set before Jesus in order to undermine his authority. When shown a coin of the Roman Empire, Jesus was expected either to endorse the power of Rome or to turn to hatred and rebellion (Matt. 22:15–22). The Pharisees, who despised Roman rule, hypocritically joined with a group of Herodians in order to ask Jesus a question, "Is it lawful to pay taxes to the emperor or not?" If Jesus were to answer "Yes," they could accuse him of turning his back on the oppression of Israel and of turning away from God as the Lord of all. If he were to answer "No," the Herodians, who had advantageous government connections, would be quick to take offense and bring charges of treachery against him. Jesus said neither "Yes" nor "No," but astounds each party by falling into neither's trap and yet satisfying both. He asks to see a coin and inquires about its image and inscription. Jesus, then, answers the question about the tax. "Give therefore to the emperor the things that are the emperor's, and to God the things that are God's" (22:21).

What is astounding about this answer? A few months ago, while helping out with a Sunday morning lesson for children, I heard a familiar interpretation of the story of the coin—one that falls completely into the Pharisees' trap. Jesus' questioners hoped that he would either reject the imperial taxes and be liable to arrest, or comply with imperial rule and, in the process, show a lack of faith in the reign of God. The teacher told the children, through a lengthy explanation and list of examples, that we give our spirit to God and our bodies and other material things over to the secular order. In fact, she said that we ought to be thankful for our government because it protects our religious expression. Does our faith need protection from the powers of the world? Does the government keep faith alive? Jesus says the opposite, and for this reason his answer was astonishing. He surprises all by reducing the rule of the great and powerful Caesar to the trivial matter of a coin. He is indifferent to Caesar, and he suggests that we should be more concerned about God.

If the coin has Caesar's name and picture on it, give it back to him; however, give to God what is marked by God. Let Caesar have his coin, but God has a claim on what is already his: the people, the land, and the entirety of creation. Caesar will make his claim, but his kingdom will pass away. We are marked by God. For those of us who carry the name Christian, the mark upon us is the name of the anointed one. We belong to Christ, and God, in Jesus Christ, shows the way for us to follow in order to take our place in the world, to be salt and light, and to take possession of the land. In God's time and in God's way the meek inherit the land, those who thirst for righteousness are fulfilled, and the peacemakers are called children of God (Matt. 5:5–9). God's way is an astonishing reversal of the world's way of doing things. For this reason, Christians give Caesar's coins back to him, but they give their lives back to God.

But, you might ask, "What about the Holocaust?" Should we stand idly by as great injustices are done? You are right; we should not. It is a matter of historical fact that war did not stop the killing of 6 million Jews and about 5 to 6 million other "undesirables." It is also clear that many lives could have been saved if Christians in Europe and the U.S. had shown hospitality to Jews. Their emigration out of Hitler's Germany was blocked at *our* borders. It is a matter of record that hospitality (particularly in France and Holland) did keep some Jews from being sent to the death camps. It is a matter of recent history that the world has stood idly by as great horrors of oppression and genocide have been perpetrated in Africa, South America, and other parts of the globe. This point is clear: if war is our means to justice, we will always be at war. "What about the Holocaust?" is a great question because it puts our imagination and our faith to the test.

In Jesus' life, teachings, and way to the cross, it is obvious that followers of Jesus do not kill in the name of righteousness, do not seek revenge, and do not put faith in the power of the sword. If we cannot kill for God, we certainly cannot do so for secular powers and governments of the world. As a matter of faith, we cannot stake our claim in the world by violence. Undoubtedly, Christ's call of peace puts us in a precarious position. Christians can be the best kind of citizens or the worst, depending upon what a government might need and require from us. Isn't it a common complaint that Christians under Nazi rule were too willing to comply with the plan of the regime? Shouldn't they have been an unreliable kind of citizens, at least in matters of war? While under an unfriendly Roman emperor, Paul instructs the Christians in Rome to "be subject to the governing authorities" (Rom. 13:1). "Pay to all what is due them—taxes to whom taxes are due, revenue to whom revenue is due, respect to whom respect is due, honor to whom honor is due" (Rom. 13:7). Paul also urges the Christians in Rome "to present your bodies as a living sacrifice, holy and acceptable to God" (Rom. 12:1). Give your lives to God, and give Caesar back his coin.

The temptations of citizenship, in ours or any nation, are either to lionize or to despise the land and the people with whom we dwell. Each option puts the history and identity of a nation at the center of things. But God is our true center. All nations will rise, fall, and pass away. It is not easy to live in a place without wanting to die for it, for those who have died defending it, and for good leaders who have the nation's economic and political interests in mind. But any place is first of all God's creation, and we are God's as well. Among Christians, the just warrior must answer to the peacemaker. Our identity, history, and shared future are shaped not primarily by citizenship in this or that country, but by God's call to us to be a people who follow Christ. This shared history and identity include people across time and the globe. We sing "America the Beautiful" because it is, indeed, a splendid countryside and the home of good and honorable people. Christians are bound to the land and neighbors as fellow sojourners. Our unity is in the reign of God.

14

Hope for the World

■ After the chapter on the nation and war, a question typically follows: If Christians will not take up arms to claim a place, can they be police officers? Then another related question: Without violence, will the world be given over to disorder and mayhem? In answer to the first question, it seems to me that Christians can be police officers as long as we (that is, other Christians) help them. Following our shared faith, we can learn to see that the world is not ordered by violence and that violence is not limited by the use of more violence.

A police officer will have an admirable career if he or she never uses a gun—except if that officer is a character on a television drama or movie. Given the popularity of violence, we might ask, "Doesn't the police officer's work depend upon the threat of force?" The answer is plainly no. If the officer's authority depends upon the use of a gun, then we are truly an uncivilized people who are in a constant state of civil war. In a world of strife and violence, additional use of force actually undermines police work (although television and movies claim the contrary). Undoubtedly, the peaceable officer will be dependent, not self-sufficient and invulnerable. He or she will not be a hero in Hollywood, but this peaceful officer will be an integral part of community life.

The peaceable officer will have to depend upon citizens who are willing to stand up for what is right, speak out, and teach their children respect for others and habits of peace. We will have to accept and share the risks of living in a violent society. When we segregate ourselves and expect that violence will stay on the other side of town, we depend upon police officers to stand between us and the violence of the world by the use of sheer force. The peace officer cannot be peaceable alone. Police shoot-outs do not put an end to gang violence; they do not make neighborhoods safe. Communities are sustained not by the imposition of force but by cooperative, nonviolent means of confrontation and hope. Violence is a response to hopelessness. Christians are called to live with hope.

Often it seems that bloodshed is inevitable and that there is little else to be done in a world of rivalry and strife. Acting otherwise in a world of conflict requires hope. We want a world of goodwill and mutual respect, but we need hope when our best intentions are frustrated. In a sermon titled "Shattered Dreams," Martin Luther King Jr. calls disappointment and frustration the "hallmark" of the mortal life. We are marked and distinguished not by our intentions and dreams, but by our failures and losses. King notes that typical responses to shattered dreams are a bitterness that turns into active hate, a withdrawal into private life, and a sense of futility that turns to despair. Hope, in contrast, leads to endurance and action toward what is good. Hope is not simply continuing on, but continuing on with faith in God's love. Hope is not merely a belief that God will provide, but also a desire to see the world as fulfilled and completed in God.

For Christians, hope has practical content. Hope gives profound meaning to acts of resistance to brutality and injustice in the world. King points out that generation after generation of slaves in the U.S. prayed and sang out for freedom in hope. They died slaves, but they sustained hope. They resisted the idea that they were meant to be slaves. In the late 1950s and early 1960s, King preached his "Shattered Dreams" to people who could have easily slipped into resentment and despair. They had been living under forced segregation, in poverty, and under Jim Crow laws for a very long time. What did King ask his congregations to do, practically speaking? He asked them to take on more burdens, to refuse to ride the bus in Montgomery for almost a full year, to be clubbed or mistreated without retaliation, to respond to their oppressors with dignity and kindness, to speak the truth, to violate unjust laws, to give their obedience to the ways of God, to evaluate their own motives, to ask for forgiveness, to see the good in their enemies, to raise their children well, to work for the good of all, to give mutual assistance, and to resist violence and injustice.

These practical steps form the "place" that Christians are called to take in the world. These little steps form a rich and wonderful place of trust, forgiveness, and generosity. The little steps are not easy, and so they require faith and hope. A venture is required, but the reward is great. I began this chapter with a question about violence and the police officer because I wanted to connect the problem of peace with the "order" of the world. Too often, we take for granted that order is dependent upon violence. Depending upon physical force seems to make good sense; the threat of force usually gets the important work of "order" done. However, we are called to hope for a different kind of order in the world. The greatest challenge to our hope is the view that patient endurance and local acts of resistance are irrelevant or futile. In hope, however, we expect that we *cannot* complete the job. We hope in the grace of God. We do not stand in our place alone, but we wait upon the Lord. People of hope open themselves to risks for the sake of striving for what is good. Unlike mere courage, Christian hope has a particular content. It begins with faith in the love of God. Our hope expresses our faith that God draws near to us in the life, death, and resurrection of Jesus. The Son is given to us, and he enters the places where we live.

Conclusion

■ A good bit of ground has been covered in this discussion of place. You may recall that we began with the utopian view of John Lennon's "Imagine." In a typically modern way, Lennon imagines a place of peace and unity that is really no place at all. His perfect place is populated by anonymous human beings. Lennon's view is representative of a modern quest for freedom and an idyllic life, which require a flight from the world, from suffering, and from entanglements of common life. It is a flight to nowhere. In contrast to this perspective, I used the theme from Part 1 of God's hospitality.

In Christ, God enters our lives where we are. Born in Bethlehem, a Judean town under Roman rule, Jesus proclaims the kingdom of God. His proclamation leads him to Jerusalem, which is at the center of God's relationship to Israel and through Israel to the rest of the world. Jesus enters the city, hailed as the son of David who was the great warrior and king. In Jerusalem, an astounding thing happens. Jesus ushers in the reign of God by suffering under the powers of the world. As he is judged by Pilate, no armies come out of the hills, and no angels descend from the heavens to defend him. The astounding thing is that God, in Christ, seeks no retribution but instead offers new life. In Jesus, God gives himself over to the world in an offer of generosity, reconciliation, and peace.

The Christian's place in the world is to see the power of God's reconciliation working in the world, to follow in God's way, and to take our place among others in the hospitality and peace of Christ. In this part of the book, I have tried to understand the Christian's place in the world in various locations—in our churches, homes, communities, and nation. In each place our role in the world requires faith and hope. In trying to live faithfully, we undertake a journey that we cannot navigate and endure alone. Indeed, we may find that we can do very little except by the grace of God, which we cannot manage and control. For this reason there is always a threat of futility and ineffectiveness in the way that we are called to inhabit and maintain our place. In this regard, the question of violence is an interesting one. Violence is a customary way of imposing order at home and abroad. Our dependence on violence is so widespread in its use that it is hard to imagine that we can do without it. The Christian role in the world is to see a different way.

In this part on "Place," I have yet to mention our care for the earth. Allow me a few words (certainly not enough) as a transition to the next part on "Things." Many in our society recognize that we are using up the earth's resources (including clean air and water) at a pace that cannot be sustained. The problems of overconsumption in the U.S. are not only personal but also part of the structure of life. We seem to have set up a conflict between nature and progress. American culture strives for a quality of life that cannot be sustained by the earth. If the majority of the world's population were to live as we do, the resources of the earth would be depleted in a matter of days. It is easy to see this situation, but solutions are harder to come by. What can I do? If I were to live a different way, things would simply carry on as before.

We produce massive and disproportionate amounts of waste, and the market for disposable products is on the rise. Our progress and efficiency divide and alienate us. I try to convince my children that a small amount of yogurt in a colorful thin tube is not only a waste of money but also a waste of plastic. They don't see my point. Regardless of one's shopping habits, the layout of our suburbs, cities, and highways requires that we consume more and more fossil fuels. We seem unable to stop polluting our water and air, and it is incredibly hard to wait and depend upon a bus. The stresses of factory farming and our hunger for chicken, pork, and beef are also too great to be sustained for long. Large-scale changes are needed, but even with the changes, it is hard to imagine that our economic vitality and our comfortable lifestyles can be maintained.

Christians are already called to a modest life with an abundance of good company. It is not a great leap from hospitality and sharing in friendship to learning to spend more to have fewer things. But to do so, we must hope. We ought to undertake small acts of living well, of preserving and caring for a place as part of our calling to friendship and peace. This is the topic of the third part of the book. We will do well to be deeply attached to things.

Part 3

Things

Introduction

■ In this part of the book, our relation to things is set in terms of the paradox of the gospel: "For those who want to save their life will lose it, and those who lose their life for my sake will find it. For what will it profit them if they gain the whole world but forfeit their life?" (Matt. 16:25–26). Here are some other paradoxes that will follow:

- Too often our possessions possess us, and a sure way to master our belongings is to give them away.
- The life of plenty is likely to make us poor, but a reserved and unpretentious way of life will bring great excess and bounty.
- Private property is a common good.
- By looking to heaven, we will take better care of the earth.
- The priceless things in our life are likely to have no monetary value.

It is with this last paradox that we will begin.

15

The Meaning of Things

■ "What are the things in your home that are special to you?" This question was put to a sampling of families in the Chicago area (in 1977). Researchers from the University of Chicago, led by professors Mihaly Csikszentmihalyi and Eugene Rochberg-Halton, were hoping to learn how Americans attach meaning to things and what our things might tell us about our lives. Family members were allowed to list a variety of objects, and the researchers cataloged and categorized over a thousand items. Furniture (excluding beds) was the most frequently mentioned category. Given the amount of time that people spend watching TV, we might expect that the television would be considered highly meaningful or useful. However, television and other kinds of passive pleasures were less meaningful because their use encouraged withdrawal from others and offered no specifically personal memories or hopes. The Chicago survey suggests that relationships and shared activities establish the significance of things.

If I were asked about special objects, I would probably list my mother's recliner, various cards and pictures our children have made, photograph albums, and several books. I say "probably" because I have already read the researchers' study, and I know that my list is typical. According to the study, children and teenagers might mention a chair or table because of its usefulness or comfort. Adults, on the other hand, usually list a piece of furniture because it represents significant relationships and formative

98

experiences. One woman pointed to two upholstered chairs and said that they were "the first two chairs me and my husband ever bought, and we sit in them and I just associate them with my home and having babies and sitting in chairs with babies." Another woman spoke of an old wicker chair that had been used for years by "one of the oldest black families in Evanston" and then given to her family. "They thought that I would take care of it. My brother brought it home. It belonged to some very special people, and it has been in the family for years." In each case, the chairs signify a shared identity, common experiences, and central relationships.

Pictures, photos, and books do the same. According to the researchers, people tend to cherish a "work of art," whether a reproduction of a famous painting, a piece from a garage sale, or a child's painting, not for its connection to "aesthetic values and experiences," but because it "refers to the immediate life history of [its] owners: reminding them of relatives and friends or of past events." Photographs tend to increase in importance as people grow older. They are regarded as "irreplaceable" because they "are the prime vehicle for preserving the memory of one's close relations." Books are treasured because they embody ideals and aspirations; they "remind people of values, goals, and achievements they seek to cultivate." The pictures, photos, and books in various households will represent widely different experiences, values, and goals. But in each case, things serve to symbolize and correspond to who we are, who we want to become, and how we live together. Our things are signs of our world.

The study by Csikszentmihalyi and Rochberg-Halton on "the meaning of things" also reveals contradictions in how we acquire, use, and keep everyday objects and tools. We may cling to things like an infant, or worse, like a child to a blanket. Things may allow us to carry an artificial sense of security or wholeness. They may arrest our relationships and growth. Certain photographs or memorabilia might be cherished because we are disconnected from those with whom we live. I might be obsessed with collecting my Elvis memorabilia or Chicago Bulls souvenirs, and in the process, live passively in relationship to neighbors and kin. What I hold dear might be a sign of a problem with my role in the lives of others.

The researchers point to such a contradiction in the use of television. By and large, Americans are attracted to television more than to any other leisure activity. According to a study, those who spend several hours a week in front of the TV "report feeling more relaxed than other times of the day." Television (like listening to popular music) functions to pacify and level their emotions. However, when actually watching TV, the same people also "rate their moods as being significantly more passive, weak, drowsy, and irritable." According to Csikszentmihalyi and

Rochberg-Halton, TV is ultimately unsatisfying, and the daily habit of watching television fosters a desire for more. The habit is a distraction from developing the kind of enjoyments that might bring even greater relaxation and sense of purpose. For Csikszentmihalyi and Rochberg-Halton, this point is critical. Passive pleasures such as television not only are unsatisfying but they also divert us from developing the kinds of attitudes, relationships, and skills that are required for engaging in fulfilling activities. Likewise, the manner by which we acquire and use things may actually undermine the meaning that we expect and hope for them to have.

Our manner of desiring and acquiring may undermine our enjoyment of things. In this regard, it is interesting that the kinds of objects that were considered special by those interviewed in the study were not new, and they were not given meaning through their market value. Old furniture, paintings, photographs, and books are likely to be worthless on the market. Even if a chair or desk is an antique, its market value is probably not a factor in its significance for its owners. In contrast, new and interesting items such as computers, video equipment, and fashionable clothes were not mentioned in the list of cherished belongings. The researchers propose that such possessions do not hold significance because they are products of year-to-year innovations. They are not owned for very long, and they do not carry a history. We do not form attachments to such new and interesting things, but to the pleasures, experiences, or new sense of self that the things will provide. If a person loves to watch TV or is attached to using a computer, then he or she is likely to upgrade periodically and take advantage of the most recent technology. If a person enjoys clothes, he or she will take pleasure in acquiring new looks and fashions from year to year, or season to season. The attractiveness of such things is the promise of new freedoms and new experiences that come with their use.

Our dominant market economy relies on a continuous acquisition of goods. We have a consumer economy that depends both on creating new kinds of products and sustaining a constant desire for more. Oddly, we seem to desire the new and the improved, but we cherish the old and familiar. We desire more power and convenience, time-saving devices, instant availability, and useful things that we can throw away or flush after their use. But we love our old hammers and tool boxes, the scratchy sound of old albums, the smell of meals that fill the house for hours, and the feel of a linen table cloth and a heavy plate. We are part of an economic process that values acquisition but fosters detachment. We are part of an economic life that requires convenience and compresses time so that we can have more freedom, but we are not usually free to "waste" or "spend" time enjoying the things we love.

At the end of the nineteenth century, Thorstein Veblen popularized the phrase "conspicuous consumption" with the publication of his *Theory of the Leisure Class*. Veblen's theory makes sense of a good bit of our acquisition and trade. He understands consumption as a form of communication through which we acquire a standing in social life. According to Veblen, we want to say something about ourselves and to gain status through our use of money. Owning things and enjoying the pleasures of prosperity have a social purpose. In Veblen's analysis, we middle-class people want to do our best to imitate the upper, leisure class and to distinguish ourselves from mere laborers. Ironically, this desire calls for a constant struggle to keep up with the Joneses. The Joneses, however, are really struggling to move upward just like us. With our eyes on each other, we and the Joneses stay relatively even, constantly needing to acquire more just to keep up.

Veblen's theory seems to make sense of consumer society's continuous desire for more, but it does not adequately explain the variety of ways that consumers want to take advantage of the market. If I were imitating the upper classes, wouldn't I be spending my money on more antiques? Veblen's theory does not explain the success of McDonald's, the shopping malls, and Disney. Dining at a fast-food restaurant cannot possibly communicate the pleasures and lifestyle of the privileged class. The theory does not explain why we might want something from Radio Shack or Circuit City, a Game Boy or a big TV, just because it is entertaining and new. The Veblen theory does not explain that our use of hard-earned money is often not for display, but to keep us isolated in our homes, or in a gated neighborhood, or far away on an exotic vacation.

The modern array of consumer goods offers not only a means for us to communicate our social standing (as it certainly does) but also a means for living out our dreams. The consumer economy is romantic. It is an exercise in the imagination. It is driven by a desire for new and enlivening experiences, and these experiences and pleasures are usually defined in stark contrast to the routines of everyday life. The consumer economy does not require that we compete with the Joneses. We may struggle instead with our boring lives. Often we seek experiences and things that will offer us an escape from the regular habits of life. Who cares what the neighbors think? A comfortable luxury car is the hard-working father's sanctuary. You work hard every day, and at home you take care of your children. You deserve the pleasure of your own insulated world and the freedom of the road.

Even laundry detergent or a spray cleaner can invigorate daily life. Gone are advertisements that reveal the shame of having a ring around one's collar or the horror of your mother-in-law testing for dust with a white glove. Who cares what they think? You have your own problems.

You have children who play hard, bleed, drool, and spill; they ruin their clothes and the house. But with quiet confidence, you can restore order and maintain a happy peace. There's no reason to scold a messy five-year-old. There will be no conflict and no toiling in the house, because cleaning is a snap. Your home is back to the way you like it.

We are not fooled by advertisements of the "new and improved." Often the product is better, and when not better, it usually is packaged differently. It has a different feel; it's worth a try. The feel of products and novel experiences are vital to the growth economy. McDonalds, the shopping mall, Disneyland, and cable television do not offer just food, wares, and amusement. They offer experiences and ways to imagine ourselves in the world. With access to hundreds of television stations, imagine the interesting options, the sports, the movies, and more. Imagine that we will be able to relax, do nothing, and never be bored. Imagine quality time we will have with our children at McDonalds, even if we do not have time to prepare a meal. The market taps into our dreams. Products need not fulfill our dreams; they need only foster our dreaming. Whether fulfilling or not, the feeling of something new is just the same.

Like *conspicuous* consumption, *romantic* consumption (that is, an economy of the daydream) is frustrating. As soon as a product or experience offers some level of permanence and becomes part of everyday life, our imagination must focus on something else—on a better world. When styles change, belts get wider, pants and shirts get looser or tighter, we are likely to desire the new things, and not because everyone else is wearing them too. On the contrary, new styles of sunglasses and such offer a look that is new and original to us. It is the novelty that is inviting. Likewise, my children want to go to Disneyland not because everyone else does, but because they have heard about that wonderful world and can imagine themselves living in it, at least for awhile. Imagine walking hand-in-hand with Goofy. The wonder of it, even for a three-year-old, will not last very long. The strange effect of modern consumption is that we are always looking beyond the world that we are in. Our economy encourages not only acquisition but also a capricious attachment to things.

In our world, market value is often sustained by an underlying sense that the meaning of things is arbitrary. My mother's blue recliner and photographs of my children are virtually worthless in the market because their meaning is sustained by interpersonal relationships and a common history. I do not think about the recliner in terms of market choice. I would not want to take it home if it were on a showroom floor. But I love the chair because of its history. In a consumer economy, such attachments inhibit growth. Our economy is healthy when things bring pleasures that become unsatisfying and meaningless over time. We must be able to dispose of things. Likewise, the meaning of things in the market is carried by a sense of new experiences and by moving forward. The irony of these temporary attachments is that we usually do not get anywhere that does us any lasting good. Like riding the Ferris wheel at the fair, we enjoy a nice view and a pleasurable ride, but when we get off we are in the place that we started—and maybe just a little bit dizzy.

We have an economy of "Ferris wheel" consumption. Just last month, I witnessed the thrill of our town's annual carnival. For our children, expectations grew to enormous proportions as they watched for three days while the rides and booths were set up in their schoolyard. For them, the rides and games turned out to be as exciting as they looked. I can remember my own childhood experiences. There is, indeed, wonder in the dizziness, and as I became bored with one ride, there seemed to be always another ride that was a bit more breathtaking. Our children were sad at the end of their carnival evening when the perspectives of parents and children diverged. The children were frustrated with the limits of just one carnival day each year. Mom and I knew that additional days would diminish the excitement, and other than simply being frugal, we were preserving the thrill of next year.

This is the irony of our Ferris wheel economy. "Wanting" rather than "having" keeps the experiences alive. In our desire for the heights and amusements of the carnival rides, we lose perspective. We lose a sense of our place on the ground. The "wanting" encourages a kind of dizziness that will be the theme of the next chapter. In always wanting more, we may be unable to see that in our acquiring and owning of things, we might be possessed by our possessions.

16

Debts and Gifts

■ Most of us are able to resist the interminable "wanting" of our consumer economy. You and I may be confident that we are not taken in by desires for social status, by dreams of invigorating experiences, or by simple fascinations of the new and improved product. Our little acts of resistance—of living without a cell phone, Internet access, cable TV, a big screen, or possibly without the television itself—will leave us out of step. To stay in step and to go on with the sense that life is getting better, one is likely to have to share the over $560 billion in credit card debt among U.S. consumers. The figure of 560,000,000,000 is the mark set in 2001, and the number has been consistently rising. Overall U.S. consumer debt was estimated at $6.5 trillion in 2001. Over the past decade, the number of personal bankruptcies has hit a new height each year (with 1.5 million filings in 2002). The lesson here, I suppose, is that our desires for good social standing and for novel experiences put our everyday lives out of balance. The "good life" is beyond the means of the ordinary person.

What, then, is a good life, and how ought we to use our property and assets to live well? Interesting answers to this question are carried by the history and tradition of the church. We often think about wealth and financial security as blessings and give thanks for them to God. However, this connection between our prosperity and God's grace is hardly the whole story. The meaning of living faithfully is tied up with what we do with what we have been given. We are called to invest rather than hide our blessings for safe keeping. We ought to risk what we have in order to see our talents and assets grow. In other words, there is an intimate connection between living well and the wise use of what we possess. The wisdom of the Christian faith may be seen as foolishness to some, insofar as we see voluntary poverty as a route to the abundance of life. In this connection, the measure of living well is God's gift of grace. The measure of our possessions is friendship with God.

In the parable of the talents, a man of considerable means is about to set out on a trip, and he entrusts his property to three servants, giving five talents to one, two talents to another, and one talent to the last (Matt. 25:14–30; Luke 19:12–27). The first two servants invest their trust and receive a good return. They double their talents. The third servant, however, buries his talent in the ground because he fears the master is a harsh man: "reaping where you did not sow, and gathering where you did not scatter seed" (Matt. 25:24). Out of fear, this servant does not recognize the grace of being trusted with a talent. In the endowment, he sees only a great burden and threat. He does not recognize the generosity of his master. In the end, this "wicked and lazy slave" (much like the unforgiving servant in Matt. 18:23–35) receives the cruel treatment that he expected from the start. The single talent is taken from him, and he is thrown out into the darkness.

The parable is usually taken to mean that we should do the best with what we have, that we should respond to grace not by turning inward in fear and insecurity, but with a venture of faith and confidence. The wealthy man tells his slave that at least, "You ought to have invested my money with the bankers, and on my return I would have received what was my own with interest" (Matt. 25:27). As a parable, the story of the talents is not meant to be interpreted literally as a lesson in investing money. However, our use of financial assets certainly applies to the story as one among other kinds of endowments or "talents." When the one talent is taken away from the wicked and lazy slave, the master gives an explanation. "For to all those who have, more will be given, and they will have an abundance; but from those who have nothing, even what they have will be taken away" (v. 29). This saying is all too true in the harsh realities of economic life. The rich get richer and the poor get poorer, and unprotected assets are often taken away. In response to the harsh and merciless realities of life, in economic matters and otherwise, we might be led by fear to hide away our treasure. But our response to the gift and talent ought to be a risk and endeavor of faith.

The parable of the talents applies not to occasional or isolated endeavors, but to the gifts and risks of a lifetime—the venture of our whole lives. The weight of this venture became clear to me when I learned that the biblical "talent" was worth more than a laborer would earn in fifteen years.

Burying the talent in the ground is not such a bad idea if one is the slave of an unforgiving master. How could a lost talent ever be repaid by a slave? The so-called "wicked and lazy slave" was concerned with self-preservation, and self-forgetfulness was the important thing for the servants who put their two and five talents to good use. They did not seek to preserve or gain anything for themselves, but instead kept at the work of their master while he was away. By doing his work, they were rewarded with the greater responsibilities of service (given charge of many things) and welcomed "into the joy of [their] master" (Matt. 25:21). The wicked and lazy slave, in contrast, is much like the rich young man who holds on to what he has and is unable to give it away and follow Jesus (Matt. 19:16–22). The two "good and trustworthy" slaves are much like the disciples, who leave their houses, families, and fields to receive one hundredfold in return. They will receive the bounty of life with God (Matt. 19:27–30).

The parable of the talents gives us perspective on how to understand "the good life" and how to use our property to live well. On the one hand, the good and trustworthy servants put their assets to work, while on the other, their work is not their own but the master's. Since the time that Christ was first proclaimed to be raised from the dead, it has been considered a sign of nearness to God that a person might willingly become poor. A person's possessions and standing are not considered things to be grasped, but are made into gifts. By contrast, the wicked and lazy slave was unwilling to risk the talent; he was unwilling to use it as the master would. If the parable of the talents is a lesson about this venture (about risking it all), we have an interesting angle from which to consider the contemporary connections between bounty, the good life, and pervasive debt.

What does our debt say about how we put our assets to use? To start, it is important to recognize that personal excess and irresponsibility are good for the economy as a whole (that is, the venture serves the one who lends). Banks and producers of goods and services are not complaining about personal debt. It is common practice among lenders to give credit cards to people who are already deeply in debt and to college students who do not have jobs or a credit history. Cautionary tales are told of twenty-year-olds who amass thousands of dollars of debt on pizzas, nights out to the movies, and weekend trips. Cautionary tales are told of thirty-five-year-olds who deal with one massive credit card debt by applying for another one. This approach to debt is not hard to understand if one remembers that some recent economic theories have been based on the same idea that the national government can make its way out of debt if people would spend more and in this way foster economic growth.

This logic of excess leads to a second point. Our dominant social and economic frameworks offer little resistance against avarice and envy. Greed and covetousness are misunderstood if they are considered simply as an excessive desire for things. In this regard, remember that it is not the extremely rich or poor who live in debt, but those in the middle who need and qualify to receive credit. Those who incur great debt may not see their lives as excessive, and they may not be strongly attached to things. They are just keeping pace and enjoying the kind of life that they believe any hard-working person deserves. In this way, greed and envy are often difficult to recognize. They are driven by a disordered desire for self-preservation. In our greed, we do not necessarily seek to be extravagant, but only desire to establish ourselves and to protect ourselves. We maintain the coherence of our lives not through our possessions, but through the power to acquire and protect our possessions. Through envy, we seek to establish ourselves in relation to others through desiring what they have. In greed, we experience loss and a threat to our well being when we are unable to acquire more things.

In the process, "the good life" is defined as having far more than a person might need to live well. A greater enjoyment of things is understood in terms of an excessive or disproportionate desire for them. We tend to want cars that can go faster than we should ever drive, and houses with empty rooms. We want economic freedom to fashion the kind of life we desire. Aristotle held that the things needed for a good life are limited, but that our desires can be unlimited. The good life, for the ancient philosopher, required self-control. We happen to live in a time when the good life is defined by the possibilities of our unlimited desires. Oddly, this unlimited desire leads a person to behave like the servant who buries his talent in the ground. He is self-absorbed and thinks only of his own fate. His use of fifteen years of wages is entirely determined by self-preservation. He seems incapable of risking his master's trust in order to do his master's work.

The effect of living to the edge of our means is self-absorption. Again, this selfishness is more likely to be a matter of fear and self-preservation than outright greed or self-indulgence, but the result is the same: things dominate our lives. To gain a measure of freedom, to do the master's work, we will have to live out of step and give up on the ordinary, middle-class sense of the good life. We will have to skip trips to Disneyland, drive rusty cars, live side by side with people who need us, and maybe even earn less money for the sake of good work. People drive old cars, borrow from each other, and walk to work all the time, and the person who receives five talents has no less grounds for living modestly than the person who receives one. Too often the five talents go to depreciating assets, to goods and services that are the modern equivalent of a hole in the ground. We are called to be friends of God's friends, and to do so, we are called to recognize and use our blessings as gifts. We will make wise investments when we put them to appreciating assets, in people and in places where we cultivate a common life.

17

Wants and Needs

■ What do we need for a good life? A common response is to distinguish what we need from what we just want or would like to have. Behind this reference to what we need is usually the idea of "what we need to survive" in contrast to merely social or cultural wants. However, this distinction is not workable. It misses the point that human beings have social needs that are essential. Take a person's food away for a day, and she will be hungry. Strip a person and make him walk about unshod and in a loin cloth for a day, and he will find it hard to function. His life that day will be a joke. As people stare or point or fain indifference, he will feel shame. He will not be admitted into restaurants or grocery stores. Without the right clothes, he may not be able to eat, or at least not be able to eat as a full member of *his* community. To this degree, "what we need to survive" is bound up with the question of what we need to survive with the respect and fellowship of our neighbors. What we need is an element of who we are in common life.

What do we need? The question is particularly complicated in a society like ours where social life is often coordinated with a consumer economy. In growth capitalism, unlimited wants are needed. Unlimited wants generate economic health overall, even though individuals might be frustrated with their unfulfilled desires and with their debt. As I have noted above, this peculiar relationship between the individual and the whole of economic life tends to give legitimacy to excess, envy, and greed. But this

108

dysfunctional relationship does not render us helpless. There are ways to resist. Most of us are able to put limits on our wants because we have other ways to understand ourselves as social beings. We share a place and a purpose in different kinds of communities. With a sense of social purpose, we can have a clearer sense of what we need.

What we need to live well is a suitable and respectable place among others, and what we need to live without shame depends upon the nature of our society and our place. Adam Smith pointed out that a laborer in his day would need a linen shirt and leather shoes. Aristotle believed that respectable citizens of Greek cities needed enough wealth to be self-sufficient, to enjoy higher pursuits of leisure, and to exercise virtues, not only of justice and temperance but of magnanimity and generosity as well. So according to one's place, whether in eighteenth-century England or in ancient Greece, a person would need certain things to live with decency and respect. I am a decent father when I embarrass my daughter by wearing black socks with my sandals; undermining current fashion is a fatherly thing to do. However, I threaten disrespect if I wear my bathing suit during a conference with her teacher. Decency and respect are in large part local matters. Our possessions reflect who we are in a place.

In a consumer economy, however, emphasis is not so much on what a person has, but upon buying power. To this degree, it is strikingly easy for a person who is immersed in market culture to experience economic anxiety. It is not possession, but the continual process of acquisition that keeps one in good standing. A lack of good standing leads to shame, and I am not certain about where American culture draws the line between good standing and humiliation. Shameless behavior can make people famous and bring them a lot of money. People make a name for themselves while singing before thousands of people in their underwear or by airing private matters in public. Nevertheless, we do have widely used terms of disgrace, such as "welfare queen" or "deadbeat dad," and it is not uncommon to hear someone state or imply that the poor are poor because they are lazy.

In the church there is no shame in poverty. Likewise, there is no shame in recognizing and admitting our own faults and moral failures. In fact, recognizing our own sins opens us to grace. We learn to stand before God as poor sinners. Ironically, if we think that we are self-sufficient, we have to learn to be ashamed and to see Christ's humiliation on the cross as a healing grace. There is shame in arrogance and self-satisfaction, but there is no shame in being dependent. It is hard to summarize the long tradition of Christian thought on poverty, but a few points are clear. First, it is shameful when the poor do not receive care and protection. The prophets announce God's condemnation on those "who trample the head of the poor into the dust of the earth, and push the afflicted out of the way"

(Amos 2:7). Poverty shames not the poor, but the rich. Second, there is dignity in providing for the ones we love—in caring for our children and parents and in looking after the saints and sinners in our everyday lives, in whom we see the presence of God.

The questions of "what we need" and "what we need to live without shame" become particularly interesting when Christians look to enjoy the company of God. Mother Teresa is one of the most notable examples in recent times. She set out to find the love of God among the poor and dying in Calcutta, and to do so, she needed only a plain sari of her own, a place to shelter the sick, and food to share. Among the outcasts of India, she found God's goodness and joy. In this part of the book and the next, I will appeal to the wisdom of Christians of the third and fourth centuries, like Synclitica and Antony of Egypt, who imagined a life of desert simplicity and poverty where they would find the abundance of God. They shed their possessions in hope that by doing so they would discover that God is all that we need. This desire is at the heart of Christian hope. I will try to apply their insights from the ancient desert to the neighborhoods of modern life.

In the spirit of hope, Synclitica headed out into the desert of fourth-century Egypt. She believed that wealth will preoccupy us (and consume us) with pleasures that are ultimately useless. She set out in hope for greater riches. To her sisters and brothers in the desert, she explained that "worldly people esteem the culinary art, but you, through fasting and thanks to cheap food, go beyond their abundance of food." Synclitica directs us to everlasting nourishment, reminiscent of Jesus' encounter with the Samaritan woman at Jacob's well (John 4:1–42). "Everyone who drinks of this water will be thirsty again," Jesus tells the woman, "but those who drink of the water that I give them will never be thirsty. The water that I will give will become in them a spring of water gushing up to eternal life" (vv. 13–14).

Christians in the ancient world were often suspicious of wealth because it cultivated and sustained the conventional distractions and sinful habits of Greek and Roman societies. Conventional society was understood to undermine common life in God. I am thinking specifically of John Chrysostom in Antioch (347–407) and Ambrose in Milan (339–397). John was a particularly relentless critic of the rich, and his public criticisms of the wealthy ultimately led to his removal as bishop of Constantinople. He did not reject money and possessions as evil, but he did hold that the accumulation of private property for the sake of private benefit was sinful. When we use wealth in a way that divides rich from poor, we defy the purposes of God's good creation. In a timely example for us, he points out that dogs of the rich eat better than many poor people. We could add that the pets of the rich have more comfortable beds and better health care as well. John held that people too easily become servants to their possessions, and by doing so, they turn their back on their neighbors.

John Chrysostom proposed that the goal of private ownership is the sharing of common life. It is the poor, not your dogs, who will stand with you before God on the judgment day. "God has given you many things to possess, not in order that you may use them up for fornication, drunkenness, gluttony, costly clothes, and other forms of soft living, but in order that you may distribute to the needy." Through distribution we become masters of our wealth. According to John, we ought to share in God's dominion, in the providence of God who gives the sunshine and the rain to all. He cites the prophet Isaiah (5:8). "Rich and poor alike enjoy the splendid ornaments of the universe. . . . Hence it was said of those who join house to house and estate to estate: 'Shall you alone dwell in the midst of the earth?' The house of God is common to rich and poor."

Ambrose, bishop of Milan, also appeals to Isaiah 5:8. Isaiah cries out against the wickedness of "You who join house to house and field to field, until there is room for no one but you." Ambrose confronts a situation in Roman society where the land is owned by a few and cultivated by poor tenant farmers. This state of affairs was perfectly legal under Roman law, but according to Ambrose, it was an offense to God. It is clear to Ambrose that God intends the fruits of the earth for all. Nature does not discriminate, but brings us all into the world poor, naked, and needy. Likewise, we will be put into the ground as equals. The bodies of both rich and poor will be reduced to dust and bones. Ambrose held that ultimately the earth belongs to all, so that the distribution of one's wealth to those in need is a way of returning a trust. Giving to the poor is not a matter of personal whim or inclination; rather it is necessary and essential to proper ownership.

For Ambrose, the offense of the rich is not their desire to possess the earth, but their desire to separate themselves from the human race through their possession of the land. The right to property is not absolute, but conditioned by our common origin and destiny as human beings. Our destiny is given by our creator, the only rightful owner of all the earth. Ambrose objects not to the possessions of the rich, but to the exclusion of the poor from sharing in the bounty. "Do spacious halls exalt you, which should rather sting you with remorse, because, while they hold crowds they exclude the cry of the poor—although it would be of no avail that this cry be heard, which even when heard gains nothing." The point is pertinent to us insofar as we enjoy the contemporary strategy of building isolated neighborhoods. Not only property values, but stone entryways, isolated streets, and suburban highways function to sustain the harmony of the self-sufficient middle class. Ambrose drives his point home: you hear the cries of the naked, but "you are solicitous as to what marbles you will use to cover your floors."

The lesson here is simple. Wealth is misused when it is a means of isolation. Money and material assets hold out a false promise of security. We can put our means to the task of protecting our lives from the vulnerabilities of poverty and misfortune, and we can build houses, neighborhoods, shopping districts, and vacation homes that provide us with a refuge and retreat from the disharmony and ugliness of the world. It is fully attainable for the American middle class to live from day to day, from home to thoroughfare, from thoroughfare to workplace, without encountering or looking upon poor neighborhoods. Urban and suburban highways allow us to drive around or above. To this degree, the use of wealth is not a matter for individuals. It pertains to how a community organizes its life. The right use of our bounty requires a community that sees no shame in poverty and recognizes the disgrace (the lack of grace) in driving past the poor.

John Chrysostom and Ambrose are part of a tradition that is not socialist in the modern sense—in the sense of state or corporate control of property. Individual or private management and charge of property is considered a good (by Thomas Aquinas) that fosters the dignity and responsibility of caring for one's self and one's family, the orderly stewardship of property, the virtue of justice, and civic harmony. Private property is good, but it is not absolute. I cannot cast the contents of my refrigerator into the backyard to rot simply because private ownership allows me to deal with food as I please. Following Ambrose, we should say that the fruits of the earth have a common destiny and purpose: to sustain human life and to sate the hungry. If good food is thrown away when people are still hungry, our economy and sense of ownership is disordered.

Property is an instrumental good that should serve the human community. On this point, John Chrysostom and Ambrose understand giving to the poor as a key sign of whether or not we have mastery over our possessions (or whether our possessions possess us). The ordering of our possessions, for Thomas Aquinas, corresponds to an ordering of love and justice. As a matter of justice, I have a duty to love, to nurture, and to educate my children. They have a claim upon me that is more intense and immediate than the claim of my neighbors and my neighbor's children. However, my neighbors and even my enemies also have a claim to live well. They are entitled to share the bounty of creation and to share good standing in common life. My specific responsibility to my children is not opposed to the needs of my neighbors. On the contrary, we have a responsibility to cultivate a modest life so that we will have enough resources left to contribute to the lives of our neighbors. This is the great privilege of having what we need. We can live with dignity among our neighbors, and use our assets to contribute to common life. There is shame in absolute ownership and isolation.

In a sense, we need much more than what we need to simply survive. Because what we need is largely determined by our place in social life, we Christians need to be part of a community that lives with a common purpose, with a shared vision of living faithfully in the society and association of God. We need to be part of a community that sees no shame in poverty and understands the disgrace of overlooking the poor. We need people who have faith in the destiny of creation, in our common end in God. We need hope so that we will not use our resources simply to create a refuge in an insecure and dangerous world. We need at least a rough picture of a good and modest life—an alternative way of living in an economy of excess and isolation. We need enough to live well and to care for our families, close neighbors, and friends. We need enough to share and to give hospitality to the stranger—to put our property to the higher use of common life. Finally, we need enough to live in such a way that we can give our money away in order to contribute to what is, economically speaking, both inefficient and useless. I will develop this last point in the two chapters that follow.

18

Work and Cultivation

◼ We have a calling to take care of things and to put them to good use. Behind any conception and use of property is a conception of our place as human beings in the world. In Genesis 1–2, God gives human beings dominion over the earth. We put our hands to creation, and we are able to give order and purpose to things for our good and the good of the creatures of the air, land, and sea. Sharing in God's image, we plan and create as God does, and with God's grace we can participate in God's very creativity and love. However, we also can resist God's grace and burden ourselves and the world with disorder. We are able to take possession of things in a way that isolates us and denies the common destiny of all creation in God. In Acts 2, the first Christians who received God's Spirit shared their possessions and cared for the poor. Their material bonds and table fellowship are signs for us of God's restoration and new creation in Jesus Christ. In Christ's bodily resurrection, we see the promise of our reconciliation and peace in the world of creatures and things.

Our dominion over the earth is certainly reason for worry. Human progress, in shaping the world to our use, has put us in a competitive relationship with the earth and its creatures. Our fossil fuels and industrial waste have polluted the water and air; deforestation all over the world has caused the extinction of countless species and has put stress on the atmosphere; our highly productive methods of farming are depleting our topsoil at a rapid rate; and our everyday lives seem to be locked into a system of overconsumption. Our progress is not growth for the earth.

Last summer, we in the state of Maryland were suffering through a long drought. Our town, like most municipalities, had imposed severe restrictions on water use. The local self-serve car wash was allowed to stay open a few days during the week. When in service, the car wash attracted a line of consumers. It was a striking scene. Amid constant worries about running out of water, we could not help washing our cars and vans. People could not manage to get through the drought with a dirty automobile or to simply rinse the car with a sponge and bucket. Many cars in the line had no visible grime or dust. The trip to the car wash seemed to be as much a ritual as a removal of dirt. Car owners displayed considerable focus on their task and an obvious sense of rhythm with the spray wand. Water washed over their automobiles like rain. People were caring for important things in their lives.

Many propose that we human beings should not consider ourselves the center of things. A few decades ago, Carl Sagan popularized this idea, and it is held by many others, like Stephen J. Gould and E. O. Wilson, who care deeply for the preservation of the earth and its creatures. According to this view, the biblical idea that we have "dominion" over the earth is one source of our abuse of the earth. In response, many conservationists think that we human beings should downplay our role and consider ourselves just one species among many. This view is contradictory, at least from the point of view of conservation. If we are just one species among many, why should we worry about species of frogs in the rain forest or the turtles in the Galapagos Islands? The frogs are certainly not worrying about us, and they would carry on happily if we were to die off as a species. Carl Sagan was right; *we* have a problem in our care for the earth, and *we* should play a role in changing they way we do business. The conceptual problem that he cannot solve is this: How do we put ourselves at the center of creation, with dominion, but still avoid a self-centered domination over the earth?

From a theological point of view, this question, at least in theory, does not present a difficult problem. However, our "dominion" continues to be a considerable practical problem. In other words, our self-centered domination over creatures and things persists as a nearly hopeless problem of sin. Theologically, we put ourselves at the center of creation only insofar as we share the image of God. God is the beginning and end of creation, and in between the beginning and end, God gives us a role in sharing divine creativity. We are able to participate in God's ordering, purposefulness, and care, right in the middle of things (on the ground floor), through our knowledge of how the world works and our freedom to do one thing or another. This theological view gives us a noble task, but it also assumes that we can do terrible damage to ourselves and to the earth as well. As I mentioned above, this theological view does not fix the practical problem, but it does change how we look at our role in creation.

If we were to love God more and to worship God with more intensity and consistency, then we and the earth would be better for it. This statement reverses the popular view that religious people cause or allow a great deal of destruction precisely because they are always looking to the heavens rather than tending to the earth. This popular accusation is not well considered. The problem with our abuse of the earth is that we do not look to heaven enough. The problem is that we have tilled the earth like a horse with blinders, looking only to what we can make of the ground. Imagine how much better our relation to the earth would be if Christians everywhere were to join Jews in setting aside a day for God's peace: no construction or demolition, no driving or shopping, and no waste billowing out of the smokestack at the plant. The economy would lose a day, but we and all the creatures of the earth would gain one.

The Christian faith (like Judaism) goes even further in its understanding of our relation to God and the earth. By recognizing that God is the creator of all, we rightfully have dominion only in relation to God. This is the fundamental point: we will not be able to exercise proper care and good order over the earth until we ourselves are set in order. In the Christian faith, we learn to call ourselves sinners and to recognize (to repent) that we cannot set ourselves in order except through God's grace. Insofar as we are disordered in our hearts and minds and in our practical relations with God and neighbor, our relation to the earth will reflect our own disorder. Until we are open to the grace and hospitality of God, we will exercise a harsh and unforgiving dominion over the earth.

In effect, the problem of our relation to creation is far worse than Carl Sagan imagined. We cannot fix the problem on our own or merely work to change the system so that people will be *forced* to change. People and communities must be changed first, and for this we hope and have faith in God's love, and we patiently wait. We often hope that God will resort to the kind of dominion that we exercise, that God will take a bulldozer to whatever stands in the way of good order. However, our Lord did not seek to establish the reign of God by force, but instead by suffering the violence of the cross. Likewise, we have been given the gift of dominion and God's offer of grace. It would be utterly inconsistent for God to bring peace and order to creation by pushing us out of the way.

These reflections on dominion and faith bring us to the point where we should consider how we are capable of putting our hands to creation and of cultivating things of the earth. To do so, I will review the proposal of Dorothy Sayers, who puts forward the idea that work is an expression of the image of God in us, that we "should make things, as God makes them, for the sake of doing well a thing that is well worth doing." The phrases "doing well" and "well worth doing" pack a whole set of arguments in a few words. We should be concerned with "what is well worth doing," that is, with work that is essentially good, like teaching, nursing, carpentry, and digging a foundation for a home. If the work is good, we should be concerned to apply ourselves to doing it well *precisely and primarily because it is good.* Nursing, masonry, and home construction have their own practical standards of good work. Sayers asks us to consider these forms of work as good in themselves, to perform our tasks with skill and care, and to apply ourselves to their purposes.

Sayers argues against external values that we might impose upon a job or career. Internal or intrinsic goods have a "built in" connection to our work, while external values are disconnected. In regard to external values, Sayers rejects money as a *guiding* purpose. She despairs when she hears people say, "I do not like my job, but I make good money." Here, money is valued regardless of (or outside of) the work. Certainly, we need to earn a living, and Sayers agrees that we deserve a just wage. However, she also urges us to be forgetful of wages during the workday. Instead, we should be attentive to the demands of our work, and if it is good work, we will be better for it. Going further, Sayers argues that we should not work merely in order to provide what we need to survive and to flourish. On the contrary, she claims that good work itself is essential to human flourishing. We need good work. Sayers also challenges the notion that we ought to seek occupations that we personally enjoy or that make us happy. She rejects this view insofar as it makes the meaning of *good* work a matter of personal preference.

To be truly fulfilling, good work needs more than a private and subjective meaning. Good work conforms to a broader conception of a life well lived. I might say, "I really enjoy selling automatic weapons because I meet all kinds of interesting people, I like traveling to gun shows, and my customers really appreciate the service that I provide." Sayers is critical of this statement on two counts. First, I appeal to my individual pleasures, and second, the worth of my work is judged according to my popularity among customers as well as supply and demand. On each point, my conception of good work is simply a matter of private preference. It is hardly possible to argue that automatic weapons do anyone in our neighborhoods and cities any good. By contrast, good teachers, playwrights, actors, accountants, groundskeepers, and plumbers do a great deal of good—inasmuch as they are good at their trade and their trade also cultivates their character.

The goodness of work applies not only to the activity but also to the person who does the work. As Dorothy Sayers puts the point, "as we are so we make." In other words, our work is expression of who we are, and from the point of view of the Christian faith, we are no less than the image of God, no less than open to receive grace and share God's creativity and care for the world. Sayers's proposal is certainly grand, inasmuch as our work takes on profound theological meaning. However, she expects that we will be doing ordinary things like laying down straight and sturdy foundations and teaching children to read. It is not the extraordinary effects that make work meaningful, but the habits and routines of applying our lives to activities and purposes in our world. With God's grace, we have the capacity to make and cultivate things and places that are truly good. In making and tending to things in the world, we cultivate human life.

19

Our Relation to Things

■ Dorothy Sayers is both an idealist and a radical. She is an idealist because she seems to have a naïve and inflated conception of our work. Does she mean to say that standing beside a machine as it cranks out plastic Happy Meal toys is good in itself? If not essentially good, does she mean to say that we should not take such jobs in order to support ourselves and our families? Contrary to Sayers's hopes, our jobs are largely instrumental. They are not good in themselves as much as they only make possible and serve other good things in life, like family, education, and leisure pursuits. Often we have a mixed assessment of our companies and employers. I might dedicate myself to the good of work itself, but the company as a whole is just out to make money. Sayers is an idealist because she assumes that we all can have the kind of jobs that are essentially and in themselves "well worth doing." She is a radical because she agrees with these criticisms. Good work requires a radically different kind of economy, a fuller conception of who we are, and modest living.

Sayers outlined her view of work while living in England during World War II. Her writing is shaped significantly by the times and the place. Sayers questions the integrity of an economy that is dedicated to war, yet she is impressed by the thoughtfulness and dedication of the workers. She is saddened by the purposes of war, but from the perspective of wartime thrift and conservation, she sees economic life in a new light. She sees that the typical modern economy (the economy in Britain before and after

119

the war) is like a treadmill in a hamster's cage. In the modern economy, we make things for the purpose of making money, and we need to consume things so that we can spend money on more things to make money. We need to need things that we do not need. The economy is driven by growth, by increases in the gross national product, the stock market, and consumer spending, but the growth does not get us anywhere. We cannot get off the wheel.

Sayers's description of the hamster cage is realistic. In our consumer economy, most jobs, especially the high-paying ones, will have no meaning except as they help spin the wheel. Third grade teachers will not be paid much. Making second graders into third graders does not put much push behind the hamster's treadmill. But if a person can move money around from one stock to another, then she is spinning the wheel hard while not putting her mark on anything at all. Nothing has been cultivated, but a good bit of money has been made.

Sayers's radical suggestion is that we think about the economy as the cultivation of human life. We would be getting somewhere if we were to draw near to each other and to God through our work. We live in a world where many of us will have to take nearly useless jobs in order to earn a living. It is, indeed, a privilege to have the kind of work that Sayers portrays as good in itself. For instance, laying brick to mortar can be a skill and a whole rhythm of life that cultivates and offers unity to a life well lived. Simply laying brick, we can apply our minds and bodies to making something beautiful, sturdy, and useful. We can put ourselves into the work and into the role we play in relation to fellow laborers. However, if we all cannot have such jobs or a role in communities where they are sustained, at least we can train ourselves to think about economic life as something far different from making money. "Making" money (unless one works for the Department of the Treasury) is a hamster cage idea. We need to "earn a living" somehow, but we purposefully enter economic life only when we do good work.

On the local level, this kind of economic life abounds. For instance, small farmers typically live differently from managers of factory farms because of their nearness to the soil and to their cows. There is a difference between husbandry and simple cattle production. The farmer undertakes an art and has great affection for the cows. The height of corn marks the rhythm of her life. Likewise, I hope that it makes a difference when my stockbroker is my neighbor. It should be clear to him that his work has a purpose when he sees the recipients of our educational funds playing in the backyard. Is the good stockbroker's work, from beginning to end, really just about money? Certainly not. Good trade, labor, and employment cultivate a common environment where friendship and hospitality are likely to grow. Economics in its fullest sense is like managing a home.

In terms of cultivating common life, meaningful economic activity is often found outside the market. For instance, many people make things only to be sold at craft shows, flea markets, and yard sales. From what I have witnessed, there is not much money in it, especially when hours and hours of work are factored into the cost. People teach night courses for pittance; they garden for enjoyment and give away tomatoes. Some parents coach soccer for free. In a consumer economy, it is often outside the dominant market where the real production is at work, where we get off the treadmill and put our efforts and skill to cultivating common life and doing good work. Recall the discussion of the meaning of things in chapter 15. Meaningful economic life is where we come into relation to old chairs, photographs, books, and homespun crafts that have no resale value. Meaningful economic life is found with hand-me-down clothes and high chairs that have been passed from family to family, generation to generation. When exchanged from hand to hand, things start to carry a history, and they shape our identities in new ways.

When off the hamster's wheel, we are free for a different kind of uselessness. The treadmill requires aimless, or at least circular, consumption and production. In contrast, Dorothy Sayers gives us the insight that work ought to be generative of something good, which is in us and in our relation to God and the world. There is an interesting excess and uselessness to the kind of work that is directed toward the goods of human life. In a monetary sense, it is inefficient with time and wasteful with resources. Many good things about work are pointless in financial terms, like the smell of pine boards, the heat of sandpaper in my hand, and feel of a smooth edge. Good work, in Sayers's sense, requires attention to beauty, to rhythm, to performance, to the contemplation of truth, to color, unity, and style, and to the feel of pots and pans.

When out of the hamster's cage, our relation to things reflects who we are, not primarily through consumption, but through our cultivation of things, places, and common life. When off the treadmill, we are likely not to use our cars or level of income as a measure of our place in relationship to others, but to see our paid and unpaid work as contributing to the whole. With this point of view, the banker encounters the proverbial ditch digger not with superiority or disdain, but with a sense of dependence and gratitude. The laborer encounters the philosopher with a sense of equality and mutual dependence. I should add that in a Christian worldview, the destitute, sick, and imprisoned also have their place. The poor, bedridden, and incarcerated are hardly useless, or I should say that they are useless in the most splendid way. They are Christ with us (Matt.

25:31–46), and by cultivating our place in relation to the hungry, suffering, and imprisoned, we draw near to the kingdom of God.

We human beings are fulfilled and reach our happy rest not through our own toil, but by God's grace. In the light of our destiny in God, we are far more than our labor and our relation to things will make of us. I think that it is appropriate to say that we have it in us to be carefree and financially unresponsive, insensitive to the pressing needs of economic advancement and cost-benefit analysis. We have it in us to be starving artists and to support starving artists, to spend less time at the work-place in order to play softball and to read, and to give our hard-earned money away to people who do not seem to deserve it. We should think hard about appreciating and depreciating assets when the master puts the talent in our hand. In an economy directed to the good of human life, our assets are found in the cultivation of arts, in sacrifice for the sake of beauty and truth, in dance, games of strategy and wit, in housing construction and other constructive labors, and in businesses that make and provide what is good for common life—not only tables and chairs, but also baseball fields, hot dogs, and cold drinks.

In view of grace and the wonder of life, we can see that our most valuable assets are things we cannot own. The possibility of using our talents and coins on things that we do not possess is truly a grace, reflects God's grace, and promises that our investments will return to us one hundred-fold. Ironically, modest living (owning and possessing less) opens the way for greater enjoyment of people, places, and things. If we own less, we are free to invest our time and resources in greater things. We are free but less secure and more dependent. We are free for the venture of common life.

A philosophical point needs to be made here. Temperate living is often confused with abstinence. Self-control in food or drink, for example, is thought to be self-denial. This view tends to consider modest living and self-control as limiting our enjoyment of things. Indeed, abstinence, such as fasting, is limiting our enjoyment of things in order to direct our desires to a higher good. By denying ourselves food, we cultivate hunger for God. Temperance works differently. Self-control makes possible greater enjoyment of things because the "self" rather than the "thing" is in control. When our hunger or thirst controls us, our relation to things and people is disordered. When disordered, our relation to things works against us. We fall into contradictions where good things, like cheesecake, stop doing us any good, and where things we own, like comfortable homes, isolate us from our neighbors.

Temperance is the virtue of putting human good at the center of our relation to things. To this degree, modest living has a direct connection to justice and grace. In terms of justice, the point is simple. Excess and intemperance put our neighbors in service to what we want to possess. Through the habits of intemperance, we begin to act as though we have no relationship to people who are not associated with things that we own. We begin to think that giving money and things away is not the logical outcome of owning them. We begin to think that charity is something extra. However, as John Chrysostom and Ambrose have indicated, we take proper possession of things when donation and shared life are an essential part of our ownership.

Modest living is not good in itself, but is measured by our openness to giving and receiving a gift. In other words, our proper relation to things is ordered by our openness to God's grace and to the love of neighbor. Grace gives awareness that we have deep needs and that we cannot complete ourselves through our ownership of things. We human beings draw near to God and creation through our need for fulfillment, so that our relationship to people and things courts a dangerous contradiction: As human beings we seek fulfillment in the world, but when we take hold of things in order to complete ourselves, our lives become disordered and we undermine our own fulfillment. Modest living is good insofar as it makes us dependent upon gifts. If we admit that we will never have enough, we will be able to enjoy things for what they can rightly offer. Living simply and without excess is not utopian, but it is a clear-sighted realism by which we accept the teaching from our Lord and believe, "Blessed are the meek, for they will inherit the earth" (Matt. 5:5).

Conclusion

■ With this call for a simple life, our treatment of people, places, and things comes to a close. In effect, these pages have been a commentary on lines of Matthew 6. In the middle of Jesus' Sermon on the Mount, the verses of Matthew 6 begin with counsel against ostentatious piety and then offer the Lord's Prayer as a model for our petitions before God. The themes of the Lord's Prayer are hope for God's ways to be lived on earth ("Your will be done on earth as it is in heaven"), our faith in forgiveness of sins, and God's help in resistance against temptations. In this third part of the book, I have taken these three themes and applied them to the second half of Matthew 6:

> Do not store up for yourselves treasures on earth, where moth and rust consume and where thieves break in and steal. . . . For where your treasure is, there your heart will be also.
>
> vv. 19–21

> Is not life more than food, and the body more than clothing? Look at the birds of the air; they neither sow nor reap nor gather into barns, and yet your heavenly Father feeds them.
>
> vv. 25–26

> But strive first for the kingdom of God and his righteousness, and all these things will be given to you as well.
>
> v. 33

"Strive first for the kingdom of God." In the fourth part of the book, we will consider the relationship between God and creation more directly and explicitly. I hope that the previous nineteen chapters about our loves and attachments have prepared the way to understand what I think is the most difficult and the most important part of the book. In the structure of the book, Part 4 marks a new beginning. Remember that the first part considered "People" so that we could begin with our situation—the situation of those of us who are American and middle class. From there, the chapters that followed, on people, places, and things, provided an attempt to see what difference God's love makes in our lives. Part 4 begins in a different place, with baptism and our confession of faith. An extended discussion of our confession of faith is necessary to underline the principle claim of the book. It is upon the logic of faith that full understanding and enjoyment of creation rests. In receiving God's self-revelation in Jesus Christ, we receive the fullness of what it means to be in the world.

Part 4

God and Creation

Introduction

■ The first three parts of this book have been ordered by a Christian conception of the love of God. Part 1 considered our love for each other as a participation in God's love for us, and Parts 2 and 3 put the meaning of places and things in terms of our love of God, neighbor, and the earth. The three parts, People, Places, and Things, form a proposal about the order and character of our loves. Implicit in the proposal is our faith that the true character of love is fostered by acknowledging and receiving God's self-giving in Christ and Spirit, and that the ordering of creation to God makes possible great love and deep attachments to people, places, and things. In other words, God's love does not require a rejection of things, detachment from people, or withdrawal from our place among others. On the contrary, the Christian life is a way of becoming deeply bound.

In Part 4, the task of the book is completed by seeking to understand our loves in terms of the Christian profession of faith. This part, "God and Creation," follows the logic of the Nicene Creed. It begins, in chapter 20, with the risk and venture that we undertake when we proclaim "We believe," and it ends, in chapter 27, with "the resurrection of the dead and the life of the world to come." With this beginning and end, the reader will see a main theme of the first three parts: our faith envisions a transformation of our bodily existence in view of our destiny in sharing life with God. Alongside this theme, Part 4 deals explicitly with God's relationship to creation. A fundamental point (perhaps the key point) is that the love of God is not found as part of the world. Certainly we find and experience the presence of God in the world, yet we are able to find God with us not because God is part of the essence of things, but because God is always active and ever-present in relation to us. Our faith in this active and ever-present relationship is what it means to say, "God is love."

129

God's love is not some substance or feeling in the world, but the sheer activity of creative self-giving expressed most freely in the life, death, and resurrection of Jesus Christ. In this regard, God's love is utterly different than human love, but in this difference we find hope and redemption. God creates and loves through grace, while we love and put our mark upon creation through our desire to be fulfilled. We can hardly reject our desires for fulfillment or our attachments and dependence upon creation. We are creatures after all. Our faith is that in following in the way of Jesus, we will find fulfillment, rest, and peace in the love of God.

20

We Believe

■ Last week, our baby, Daniel, was baptized. It was wonderful. For various logistical reasons, we waited until he was seven months old, and Daniel's age brought a level of awareness and daring that turned out to play a role in the event. He is still very much a baby, but he is able to sit up and grab, laugh, babble, and yell. It is amazing how quickly he can target and try to take hold of a hot cup of coffee or a paring knife. He benefits from our constant underestimation of his reach and determination. Old enough to take secure hold of something yet too young to judge weight, size, and proportion, he is on a mission to pull the world into his mouth. During his baptism, Daniel smiled, lunged, and drooled happily in his godfather's arms. His intentions—or mixed intentions—were clear. He vacillated between reaching to take hold of those of us around him and struggling to splash around in the baptismal pool. With or without us, but preferably with us, he wanted to go into the water.

While Daniel enjoyed wide-eyed interaction with the people gathered around him, children hung on to the edges of the pool and dipped their hands into the flowing water. They could not resist. The baptismal pool was made of two bowls connected and set at different levels, so that water could flow from one to the other. The bowls were sizable, about two feet across. From the perspective of our five-year-old son, it was a waterfall. In a whisper, he told me so, and then I could see that he was instructing his three-year-old brother likewise. Quin, our five-year-old, takes such instruction quite seriously and frequently relays important facts about the world, while his brother Jack nods in agreement and complete understanding ("Yeah, I knew that"). After the baptism, we took time to remember and discuss each of our children's baptisms and the meaning of baptism itself. What we discussed and what they understood are probably completely different. I suspect that Jack was still thinking about the waterfall. Minute by minute it was growing larger in his mind.

As we inquire about our creedal "I believe," it will be helpful to look more carefully at the child's point of view. On one hand, we have Daniel's instinctive desire to take a plunge, and on the other, Jack's imagination of baptismal water as a vast river falling from a great height. Both points of view imply that the grace of baptism is both breathtaking and life-giving. To say "We believe" suggests that the love of God has made this kind of impression upon us. To believe is to trust and to know that something is true. To believe is to be certain without seeing (John 20:29). Yet, to believe is to *see* the movement of God's grace in the world. For Christians, to confess belief in Jesus Christ is the beginning of *thinking* through God's relationship to the world. Like Jack's waterfall, our confession of faith envisions the magnificence of grace, and like Daniel's plunge, "to believe" requires the considerable risk of abandoning ourselves to the love of God.

The Gospel of Luke tells about an occasion when children were gathered around Jesus:

> People were bringing even infants to him that he might touch them; and when the disciples saw it, they sternly ordered them not to do it. But Jesus called for them and said, "Let the little children come to me, and do not stop them; for it is to such as these that the kingdom of God belongs. Truly I tell you, whoever does not receive the kingdom of God as a little child will never enter it."

Luke 18:15–17

For most of my life, I have interpreted this passage to mean that we should have the innocent and intimate faith of children. I worry about this interpretation because it easily leads to the notion that we ought to have blind faith, and "blind faith" often leads to the idea that faith is irrational and blind to "how things really are." Does faith require that we become blind? On the contrary, our faith in Jesus Christ is the basis for seeing—for envisioning, truthfully, our relation to people and our place in the world.

Following a typical reading of Luke 18:17, "receiving the kingdom of God as a little child," I used to picture the disciples as stuffy attendants who want to keep the noisy children away. The disciples see them as an interruption. They assume that the children do not belong by Jesus' side. Jesus, in contrast, puts the children at the center of things. According to this common interpretation, the disciples' formality is rejected in favor of the naïve faith of the child. As I have gotten older, I have come to have a special interest in this interpretation since I am a theologian and teacher, which means that I tend to think too much and think that others do not think enough. Bear with me as I come to the defense of the disciples. By taking the disciples' side, we might see "the faith of children" and our "We believe" in a different way.

Rather than beginning with the assumption that the disciples are absolutely wrong, let us take for granted, at least for the sake of argument, that the disciples were right, that the children did not belong on Jesus' left and right knee. Beginning this way, Jesus' teaching about children looks a bit different and fits well with the parable of the Pharisee and the tax collector, which precedes Jesus' encounter with children (Luke 18:9–14). This new way of understanding the disciples puts stress on how we receive the kingdom of God. The story of Jesus and the children becomes not so much about the faith that the children have, but about the "standing" that they lack. Jesus' encounter with children reveals not naïve faith, but the hospitality of God.

The parable in Luke 18:9–14 introduces us to a Pharisee who is praying in the temple. With his eyes upon a tax collector, who also is praying, the Pharisee thanks God that he is "not like other people: thieves, rogues, adulterers, or even like this tax collector" (v. 11). At the close of the parable, Jesus notes that the Pharisee is wrong to trust in his own righteousness, "for all who exalt themselves will be humbled, but all who humble themselves will be exalted" (v. 14). Although wrong in this regard, he is right in another way: it is good that he is not a thief, scoundrel, or tax collector. The first Jews and Christians to hear the parable would have agreed. Tax collectors were instruments of Roman imperialism. They made their living through a form of extortion, and they were a key means to put a conquered people into service to Roman rule.

The tax collector has little in common with the children who gather around Jesus, except that this repentant tax collector had the impertinence to enter the temple to pray. Like the children, he is liable to be shooed away. Parables often recount everyday events and bring them to a surprising conclusion. Likewise, the actions of the tax collector fit with the everyday expectations of his contemporaries: "The tax collector, standing far off, would not even look up to heaven, but was beating his breast and saying, 'God be merciful to me, a sinner!'" (v. 13). The parable is effective because the tax collector is right. He should beat his breast. He has no business standing tall in the temple. He is a disgrace.

If we understand this point, we are able to witness the surprise. The tax collector is the example of faith.

The idea that tax collectors are contemptible might be too distant from us. In our time, most would agree instead that white-collar criminals should approach God with similar expressions of humility. Imagine that a person uses his or her privileged economic position to extort money from ordinary people. Do we rejoice when we see this person in church, standing tall and unrepentant, with fine clothes and poetic prayers? I suspect not. We are inclined to criticize the hypocrite and elevate ourselves. Even if the criminal were beating his breast, we might say, "Thank God I am not like him."

In our day we ought to think about the tax collector as a person about whom we are inclined to say, "Thank God I am not a sinner like her." For the modern reader of the parable, the reprehensible person is usually the Pharisee. As a child raised in the church, I have learned to imagine the Pharisee as a man of fine clothes and poetic prayers who uses his privileged religious position to engage in the spiritual extortion of ordinary people. I learned to identify with the repentant tax collector. I learned to see the Pharisee as the sinner, and I have thanked God that I am not like him. If you have learned to think of the Pharisee as I have, beware. The best way for us to play the modern day Pharisees is to think that we are better than him, to think that we have escaped the lesson of the parable. When we think to ourselves, "At least I am not like the Pharisee who thinks that he is better than a tax collector," we have joined him.

The same parabolic twist holds for Jesus' hospitality to children. When we are quick to judge the disciples as stuffy and doctrinaire, we may be missing the point. In the passage, the contrast between disciples and children is not between formal adherence and naïve trust, but between those who merit a place beside Jesus, as the disciples do, and those who do not. In our times, the situation of children is similar. Children are usually considered a wonderful diversion and joy. But when children are received, productive activities and conversations pause. Work stops. In the very pleasure of receiving children, there is a clear indication that they do not belong. Sooner or later, they will have to be sent home so that important and productive activity can begin again. Even when visiting a home, children are either sent off to a playroom or monitored closely around valuable things. In this regard, children are asked to enter the adult world with reserve and with their childlike inclinations under control.

Children respond to hospitality in different kinds of ways. When invited into a new place or among adults, some children hold back while others charge ahead. Whether a child hesitates or jumps forward seems to depend upon the child rather than the situation. Sitting in Jesus' lap or on the lap of some other stranger would not make much difference for most children. Other factors—whether the child is hungry or tired—seem to be at work. When they receive gifts, they sometimes do so with great joy. However, children are just as inclined to toss the gift aside without another thought. I have been embarrassed more than a few times when my own children have received gifts with indifference or with declarations of distaste.

Is this how we are to receive the kingdom of God—with the indifference or rudeness of a child? By welcoming the children, Jesus does not comment upon the quality of their faith, but he does undermine the contrast between those who belong with him and those who do not. The tax collector and the children are not on the guest list. They are not productive or contributing members, but they are offered hospitality nonetheless. Imagine that the disciples were receiving wisdom from their teacher. When the children enter, the teaching stops abruptly. Who wouldn't shoo the children away? Like the tax collector, children are likely to enter a place boldly and are often seen as impertinent. Like the children before Jesus, the tax collector enters the temple without the proper "standing" before God and neighbor. Perhaps, if we "receive the kingdom of God as a little child," we will be able to see through the eyes of the tax collector who puts himself at the mercy of the boundless grace of God. Perhaps we will see grace flowing in the world like an immense sea or vast waterfall.

We are all children in relation to God. Some say that infant baptism is inferior to adult or believer's baptism because a small child is unable to make a choice or commitment of faith. On the contrary, infant baptism is representative of our faith, insofar as God always comes to us regardless of our immaturity and naïveté. It is presumptuous to hold that we choose God or that we merit grace, or that we give faith life within us through our own decisions. To receive the kingdom as a little child is to enter into a place that we do not make, do not merit, and do not control. To be a child is to be shaped by the world in which we are raised. To be children of the kingdom of God is to be formed into God's people in the world. To say, "I believe," is to begin a process of growth, of maturing in thought and action, and of "living into" the ways of God.

To "receive the kingdom as a little child" is to come with nothing but a capacity to be formed into God's world. Likewise, the tax collector brings nothing to the temple but his repentance—his openness to be turned around. The mistake of the Pharisee, in trusting his own righteousness, is to think that God's work with him is done. When we look down at the Pharisee, we often do the same. We think that he has a long way to go, and we forget that we also must follow God's way. To confess, "We believe," is to follow and to be formed, to be shaped by the love of God.

135

On the day of Daniel's baptism, I stood over the baptismal pool, surveying the scene with my trained theological perspective and my clear grasp of events. As parents, my wife and I had made a decision to have our child baptized, and we were seeing it through. I certainly do not want to romanticize the perspectives of my children and the other children gathered with us. There is no virtue for adults in infantile or childish faith. However, I do need to learn to see Daniel's baptism and my own through the eyes of children. To Quin and Jack, the baptismal pool was living water. The water itself was alluring, and they could not help but reach out for it. I imagine that from Daniel's point of view, he was being dipped into an ocean. Baptism is the beginning of our lives, and in the beginning we are all babes washed in a sea of grace. We live and stand upon a gift, and if this is the case, then the best response is to follow Daniel's impulse and to plunge in. Our faith is a venture that will change our lives. This is what it means to say "We believe." To profess "We believe" is to boldly take our place in a world where we see that God is the Creator of heaven and earth.

21

One God, the Father, the Almighty, Maker of Heaven and Earth

■ "I believe in God" is a statement of faith. It implies that we take our place as creatures in relation to our Creator, and that we are open to being formed in God's way of reconciliation and redemption. Our confession of faith is also the beginning of "thinking through" who we are in relation to God and the relationship of God to the world. The first three parts of the book focused on being formed in the way of God's hospitality. From this point on, we will attend primarily to the task of thinking through our faith. I say "primarily" because our thinking cannot be detached from the way of discipleship. With our eyes on this way, we will try to understand our words better. What do we mean when we declare our faith? Our inquiry about words will begin with both the simple and the puzzling—with both "God" and "love."

God is love. The simple equation of God and love is undoubtedly true, but it is impossible to fully understand and, in the end, not very useful by itself. The problem with "God is love" is certainly not God, but the fact that "love" can mean so many things. Throughout my life I know that I have used the word love in countless ways and situations, and I have said "I love you" to a sizable list of people for a number of reasons and in a wide variety of situations. My wife, for instance, is not the first person to whom I said those binding words. When I was eighteen, I fell deeply in love and said "I love you" to a young woman with the full force of heartfelt commitment. "I never want to leave your side; I cannot live without you." Always and forever lasted for about six more months. I was crushed. I really did wonder how I would go on without her. But several years later I was repeating the same words to my wife, and my first love was just a name and a story to tell. What does love mean when it can fade away so quickly? What kind of love is God's love if it is steadfast, faithful, and true?

Bridget, my wife, is wise. A few months after we started dating, I started bombarding her with "I love you." In my view, each declaration was well timed and articulate, but each time I received little in return—perhaps an "Oh, well, thank you," but sometimes just an "Oh." I was hoping for a return on my investment. I was not simply expressing a feeling; I was staking out (perhaps scouting out) territory. I was willing to take a risk, but not really. I said, "I love you," but what I meant was, "This, Bridget, is where I stand. And where are you?" Bridget's refusal to respond in kind did not come out of a dating strategy or an attempt to teach me something about love. She simply trusts words far less than I do. Her wisdom is her patience. She needed to live the words before saying them. On one occasion, I caught her off guard and managed to smuggle in another "I love you" without the usual reinforcements (the usual well-timed articulation). To the surprise of us both, she responded with, "I love you, too." Gaining her composure and without skipping a beat, she let me know that she also loves pizza and chocolate and the Kansas City Chiefs and going to the beach and a good, long nap.

Along with the many meanings of love, a basic problem with "God is love" is our frequent and (we should probably admit) inevitable distortions and manipulations of love. Obviously, my "I love you" for Bridget, not to mention the loves that preceded her, had several meanings at once, and not all of them are clear to me even now. Was I using "I love you" in a maneuver to control her love for me? The trouble with understanding God's love is far more pronounced because we are—in a word—human. We are unavoidably invested in our gifts of love. Our love for others is the manner through which we grow. At the very least, by loving another we are able to become a more loving person. The love of God is entirely different. God's love for the world does not make God a better person, fill a gap in God, or bring God to some loving state.

God loves in an entirely different way. The Gospel of Matthew gives us this teaching from Jesus' Sermon on the Mount:

You have heard that it was said, "You shall love your neighbor and hate your enemy." But I say to you, Love your enemies and pray for those who persecute you, so that you may be children of your Father in Heaven; for he makes his sun rise on the evil and on the good, and sends rain on the righteous and the unrighteous.

Matthew 5:43–45

This love is peculiar. A great obstacle to loving in this way is that it does not seem to work. In the particular situations of everyday life, such a teaching seems to be at cross purposes with accomplishing good things. The very nature of an enemy is someone who is getting in our way, especially when we are trying to do what is good: to make the office more orderly, the work line more productive, the neighborhood more considerate, our children happier, and the world better and safer for everyone. It is common to pray "for" our enemies, but praying "for" them usually means hoping that they will get out of our way.

The love of our Creator, who "makes his sun rise on the evil and on the good," seems inefficient and requires too much patience and sheer trust. When will such a God put an end to evil and let the sun rise on the good alone? I suspect that in seeking to do good we are *not* likely to ask, "Who is this incompetent Creator who sends rain on the righteous and unrighteous? Isn't that counterproductive?" My guess is that most of us do not question God in this straightforward way. The problem is more subtle. We want to improve things and to do the right thing, so we work hard to get the obstacles (our enemies) out of the way and to move forward. Unwittingly, we may be trying to push God out of the way as well. In contrast, one mark of the saints, from the desert fathers to Mother Teresa, is a profound sense of how little we can do. Solanus Casey (1870–1957), a Franciscan from Detroit, used to say that "God condescends to use our powers if we don't spoil His plans with ours."

The plan of God, our Creator, is a plan of love. It is a declaration of God's love when we Christians confess, "I believe in God the Father Almighty, maker of heaven and earth." It is common today to use marriage as an ideal of self-giving love. According to Ephesians 5:21–33, the "one flesh" of husband and wife is an image of the unity between Christ and the church. The image of a man and woman as parents is less popular but more valuable when considering the love of God as Creator. Parenthood requires a great deal of sacrifice and self-giving. It is astounding what parents will do for their children. As a college professor, I witness parents making great sacrifices to provide their sons and daughters a good education and a safe, healthy environment in which to become an adult. Why? The answer does not have to go any further than "because they love their children and want what is best for them." Educate, guide, nurture, love, and provide; these are what parents do, simply because they are parents. Doesn't this love reflect God's providential care?

Parenthood is an interesting analogy also because (like marriage and romance) it includes a host of complications and mixed motivations. Our children reflect who we are, what we hope for, and who we want to be. For me, fatherhood has been a heavy dose of pride mixed with an even greater dose of humility. On the one hand, I am gratified and pleased with myself. We have wonderful children. I see their kindness. I see their ability to care for one another and to put their own interests aside. In their bumps and bruises, I see their daring and delight in life. I like to think that I see the best of myself in how they were raised. On the other hand, our children also do a good job highlighting my shortcomings. When they are in foul moods, they will scold each other with my words, tone, and inflection. I hear how harsh and unforgiving I can be. In hearing them, it is clear to me that I have a long way to go and that I have not raised them as well as I could. The irony of parenthood is that in raising children we have even greater opportunities to grow and to discover ourselves anew. Precisely because parenthood requires self-giving, we are given possibilities to be fulfilled in ways that we would not expect.

Such fulfillment is not necessary for God. God is complete and changeless, and this difference between God and us makes all the difference for how we understand the love of God. As a father, I cannot help but be changed by my children, and hopefully I will grow and find a measure of fulfillment in raising them. Marriage and parenthood constitute a large part of living out the course of who I am called to be. In contrast, God's activity of creation is utterly uncalled for and unfulfilling for God, who is already the fullness of existence. I use the words "uncalled for" and "unfulfilling" in particular ways. They tell us both about our relation to God and about the relationship between the Father, Son, and Spirit. A "call" sends us forward and gives us purpose, and the call to be faithful and holy is fulfilling for us because we are completed in God who gives life. In distinction from us, God is the giver of life and purpose. Creation is uncalled for and unfulfilling because God does not need or gain anything from it. We are not useful to God. Creation is grace.

The Christian doctrine of God's immovability and changelessness is frequently criticized because, its critics claim, God turns out to be a distant "prime mover" who is completely disengaged from creation. These critics propose that God is influenced and affected by creation, that the divine life is incomplete and in process. The proposal is appealing. It points to the theological problem of how to understand God's passion and love, God's movement toward and in relation to us and to all of creation. The idea of "God in process," however, creates more problems than it solves. It puts divine life *in* the process of time and development, and makes God dependent upon the development of creation. If such is the case, God's relation to the world is characterized in one of two ways: (a) The course of creation can make God into something that God must passively accept, or (b) God must control and govern creation out of self-interest, in order that the divine life might properly come to completion. In each case we are in a situation of competition with God, unless of course our activity in the world is always good for God (and wouldn't that make us gods who do not need God?).

Because God is complete and not developing in the process of time, God is continually, immovably, and changelessly drawing us near in love. This steadfast love is revealed in time. God blesses Abraham and announces "I Am" to Moses. In love, God raises up the Hebrew people to be a light and blessing to the world. To Abraham, God reveals that "I will make of you a great nation. . . . In you all the families of the earth shall be blessed" (Gen. 12:2–3). At Sinai, Israel is gathered and called to be God's way. "The whole earth is mine, but you shall be for me a priestly kingdom and a holy nation" (Exod. 19:5–6). When Israel strays, God raises up the prophets to call the people back, so that the Lord's house will be "raised above the hills" and "all the nations shall stream to it. . . . [to] walk in his paths" (Isa. 2:2–3). Amid the changes in human history, there is constancy to God's activity, bringing creation to its fulfillment in divine love.

Jesus Christ is God's way of love in time. The Christian doctrine of the Trinity, of God's unity as Father, Son, and Spirit, has developed through centuries of careful scrutiny and argument. In the first centuries of Christian history, the first set of debates dealt with the immeasurably difficult task of understanding how Jesus as a human being is "one in Being" with the Father. The divine and human in Christ are distinct yet inseparable, so that in this one person there is a unity with the divine nature and a distinct yet inseparable unity with the human nature. In this way, we say that Jesus Christ grows, changes, and suffers on earth, while God, strictly speaking, does not. Jesus suffers as a human being, and his humanity is inseparably united with, but is not the same as, his divine nature.

This mystery of union in Christ is the possibility of our reconciliation and sharing in life with God. To be with God, we need not be made into gods. In Christ, we human beings are invited to share in the divine nature (2 Peter 1:4). We are not annihilated as humans or absorbed into the divine, but redeemed and made participants in God's life. We share in God's love as distinctly human beings. This sharing is possible because the man who weeps beside the tomb of his friend Lazarus is the Son of God who has the power to raise him from the dead. Jesus who suffers the pain of persecution and rejection is the incarnate God who need not suffer, but suffers as a human being out of love.

The astounding revelation of the cross and resurrection is that God does not passively accept the human course of things. God is not distant and helpless, as in option (a) above, and does not govern or control creation

141

out of a desire for fulfillment, as in option (b). Jesus responds to violence, to envy, to the military might of Rome, and to the powers of the world not by resorting to violence and domination but by taking the place of a criminal and suffering a shameful death. From this lowest place, God brings life. Jesus' passion and resurrection are God's active response of hospitality. Jesus Christ is God's offer of grace—not for God's own fulfillment but simply because God is God. Here I am looking back to the question I asked earlier about parents: Why do parents sacrifice, nurture, provide for their children? They do so because this is what parents do—simply because they are parents. Likewise, Jesus does not resist evil, but returns evil with good, not for ulterior motives or as a means to some other end, but because that is what the incarnate God, the Son of the Father, will do.

In the Nicene Creed we Christians confess that Jesus Christ is "one in Being with the Father" and "through him all things were made." As architect and maker of all creation, Jesus Christ announces the kingdom of God. In Christ, the kingdom comes "on earth as it is in heaven." In inaugurating the kingdom, Jesus gathers the lame and the blind; he eats with sinners and draws near to the leper. He calls an end to retaliation, and he teaches about practices of forgiveness. All of these things, along with his suffering and death, do not change God, but reveal the changeless divine will of the Creator. Jesus Christ reveals how "things were made," and for this reason we Christians are able to see that God's activity of creation is God's love. Our loves too readily draw us into competition with our enemies. We struggle with those who resist our good. The astounding thing about divine love is that there is no reason for God to resist us, even though we are often set against God. When we confess that Jesus Christ is "one in Being with the Father," we acknowledge that following in Jesus' way brings the fullness of life and reveals the hardly imaginable grace of God who sends the rain on the just and unjust.

When I was eighteen, my "I love you" was the product of immaturity, and today when I say the words to my wife and children, I am deeply and sometimes painfully aware of how much I need to learn about those words. I try to say them at moments of reconciliation, when our failures are out in the open and we are setting out in the right direction again. For you and me, there is a difference between who we are now and who we have the potential to be. Along the way, we can point to achievements and failures, what has been completed and what needs to be done. For God, there is no such distinction between potentiality and activity, between potency and being. God is complete. God is the continuous movement of love. For this reason it is inaccurate to refer to God's act of creation, as if God were done with us and is now receding or moving on to something else. God's ongoing activity of creation is the outward flowing of life, which makes us and meets us as pure hospitality and grace.

For God, Creation Out of Nothing, and for Us, Lots of Things

■ The stars, the mountains and waters of the earth, and the creatures, plants, and elements of the soil, water, and air are so vast in number and type, and so ingenious in design and function, that we often overlook the simplicity of God's creation. "Then God said, 'Let there be light'; and there was light" (Gen. 1:3). With the utterance of the command, it is done: "Let it be . . . and there was." With the same simplicity, God commands the earth to bring forth life. "Then God said, 'Let the earth put forth vegetation: plants yielding seed, and fruit trees of every kind on earth that bear fruit with the seed in it.' And it was so. . . . And God saw that it was good" (Gen. 1:11–12). Because the command is direct and absolute, we may be tempted to think that the majesty of our Creator is akin to the power of a president, emperor, or king, with a multitude of people and resources at his disposal and with armies at his command. We may miss that God is simply God, with no minions to carry out the task of creation. No servants or slaves are created to tend to God's needs. God creates through peace.

The phrase "simply God" is misleading if it implies that God is lonely and needs to make himself a companion. It is strange for us "simply" to

143

exist and survive because the mere necessities of life are a constant concern and need continual replenishment. Because we are part of creation, God simply as God is unimaginable. In the very first verses of Genesis, those who compiled and recorded the story of creation encounter this difficulty of describing the indescribable. "In the beginning when God created the heavens and the earth, the earth was a formless void and darkness covered the face of the deep, while a wind from God swept over the face of the waters" (Gen. 1:1–2). A "formless void" is described and then immediately filled in with "the earth was"—with the deep, the wind, and the face of the waters. Despite this premature description of the void, it is clear from the activity of God's creation, from the simple "Let it be," that God does not need the wind and waters but can simply call them into existence. Nothing needs to be used, consumed, or transformed. God creates out of no things. From nothing, everything is created by God who is, unimaginably but simply, uncreated.

The significance of God's activity of creation as it is presented in Genesis 1–2:4 becomes clearer through its contrast to alternative accounts of creation, particularly the *Enuma elis* ("When on high"). The *Enuma elis* is a creation epic of the ancient Mesopotamians. In the beginning of this epic, gods of various powers and splendor are born from the primordial gods, Apsu and Tiamat. Soon the activity of the younger gods becomes an affront to their mother Tiamat, and a conflict ensues. The primordial god, Apsu, is vanquished by Ea who builds a dwelling upon him. Soon, Ea and his wife bear a son Marduk, who is born in the slain Apsu's heart. Later, when Tiamat rebels against the rule of Ea and the other gods, it is Marduk who finally defeats her. With his victory, Marduk alone rules all. He splits Tiamat in two and creates the heavens with one half and the earth with the other. He gives order to each, and assigns the gods to their places and functions. Finally, Marduk permits the killing of Kingu, who was the principal instigator of Tiamat's rebellion. From Kingu, the gods make the human race to toil in service to them, so that they will be free from the burdens of the earth.

In *Enuma elis* and Genesis 1–2, the purposes of creation and the place of humanity are remarkably different. In *Enuma elis,* the earth itself is the remains of a slain god. The creation of heaven and earth is the outcome of war. One god rises above the others, and in turn, the lesser gods create and subjugate the earth. In Genesis 1, the heavens and the earth come into being through the outward movement of God's word, "Let there be light." The earth and its creatures are created without rivalry and conflict, and human beings are created in the image and likeness of God. Humankind is given dominion over the creatures—"over the fish of the sea, and over the birds of the air, and over the cattle, and over all the wild animals of the earth, and over every creeping thing that creeps upon the earth" (Gen 1:26).

> So God created humankind in his image,
> in the image of God he created them;
> male and female he created them.

v. 27

Sharing in God's image, we take part in the ordering and ongoing life of creation. We are astoundingly useless to God, but yet central to creation. We are created not for servitude, but to be sons and daughters in the household of God's creation, where we are called to fashion a good home—to rest as God rests and to enjoy community with God.

Our role in creation not only reveals the image of God in us, but our profound dissimilarity from God as well. Put differently, our route to God and to taking our place in the life of God is entirely different from God's life in us. While God creates freely, without need of creation, created things are necessary and useful to us. We are creatures, and our place and use of creation makes us who we are. This point underlines what has been a basic question of this book. How do we find our place in creation in a way that leads us to the uncreated God? God's good creation makes us who we are, but things of the earth, dollars and automobiles, living rooms and engagement rings can distract us and destroy us as well. Rejecting it all might be courageous, but detachment from the world is at least as dangerous as attempting to make a fortress of things. If we claim to not need things of the earth, would we be holding ourselves up as gods?

C. S. Lewis once noted that it is clearly wrong to say that we are more truly ourselves when we are naked. The clothes that we wear from day to day, at home and on the job, to school and gathering to worship, communicate how we want to take our place in relation to others and reveal important aspects of who we are. On a college campus, it is interesting to see how various faculty members position themselves in relation to their role as teachers. Some wear business suits, some "business casual," some sneakers and jeans, and each will have a theory of education and a sense of the relationship to students to match the outfit. Business suits mean business; ties or skirts elevate the atmosphere of the classroom, and jeans get down to the students' level.

Likewise, our houses, yards, driveways, fences, toys, tools, cell phones, cars, trucks, lawnmowers, digital cameras, CD players, jewelry, haircuts, and tattoos all play important roles in forming and expressing our identities, and in contributing to how we understand our place among others and our purposes. This deep connection to the things of the world is both a blessing and a curse. Our relationship to creation is a blessing when ordered to God and a curse when things subtly overwhelm us. We take our place among our fellow human beings, joining together in common life and friendship, largely through the things that we share, own, and pass between us, and through the things that, together or alone, we use to spend our days. We put our mark on the things of creation, which in turn shape how we inhabit our world and share life with our friends.

Many would disagree with this deep connection between people and things. Many would want to distinguish personal identity from objects of possession and from the regular human habits of utilizing things. I would remind my interlocutors that the rejection of fashion is itself a fashion statement. The very reason that a person might wear hand-me-down or secondhand shoes is because they fit her; that is, they do not simply fit her foot, but who she is as well. She is a person who will argue for comfort, thrift, and "fittingness" over fashion in shoes, or for economy and against extravagance in everyday matters of life. The very reason a young man dyes his hair blue, I suppose, is because he wants to stand *apart* from the crowd and at the same time stand *with* those who are intrigued and delighted with blue hair. The reason that people use their money to buy spacious houses in friendly neighborhoods, good-looking and reliable cars, time-saving appliances, interesting amusements, and adventurous vacations is because these are the pieces of a lifestyle that they desire.

As creatures (unlike the Creator), we are completed in creation. Our lifestyles—our standards of living, our enjoyments, routines, and the activities through which we make friends, operate as family, and engage ourselves in community—shape who we are. If not, then what does? If not, then we are attempting to take on a godlike detachment from the world we inhabit—from the things that surround us and the uses of things (at home and work) that dominate our time.

Parade magazine recently carried a story on the new family car, "Our Home Away From Home" (January 5, 2003). "It's a combination breakfast nook, entertainment center, changing area and chat room." The *Parade* story functions as a marketing tool. Various automobiles are listed with their prices, advantages, and options. The new Pontiac Grand Prix has a trunk big enough for a nine-foot ladder, and the Dodge Ram, a heavy-duty pickup, is available in a four-door cab model for $29,000. The selling points in the article are personal choice, and each choice becomes an individual family's expression of its character. "Whatever type of family transport we choose, its essential purpose is the same: to bring us together." Family therapist Carleton Kendrick explains, "The family car still must meet the demands for practicality and safety, but it doesn't have to be boring anymore. Now it's a statement of how a family defines itself." It is striking how plainly the connection between an automobile and personal identity is made.

The connection between the family car and the home speaks volumes about how our culture imagines both the family and home. For many of us, our means of transportation has become a home, and our households have become a kind of passenger terminal, where we wait impatiently for the next trip out. There seems to be a constant effort to get somewhere and very little peace. Our home on wheels might be made "to bring us together," but there are very few seats available. There is no room or time to pick up strangers and friends along the way. If we find these connections between our automobiles, our homes, and our identities disturbing, we will certainly be able to find a car that defines us in an alternative way—as people who do not care about the connection between our identities and our cars. We might set about to find such a means of transportation, but when this issue is settled, a basic struggle will remain. How will we take possession of things? How will the things of creation shape us? How will we make use of God's good creation? How will we fashion a home, as it was in the beginning, created through God's hospitality and peace? These are the questions of our love for people and places and things.

23

One Lord, Jesus Christ, the Only Son of God

■ Part 1 raised the question of Jesus' homelessness. This theme needs to be developed further as we think through the lordship of the Son of God. When the question of Jesus' place among us comes to mind, we will find persuasive reasons to think that he has no home or is not at home in the places where we dwell. In Matthew 8, Jesus is in Galilee, where "he cast out the spirits with a word, and cured all who were sick" (v. 16). Who is this man? It is not surprising that a would-be disciple (a scribe) declares that he will follow Jesus everywhere. But Jesus rebuffs him, "Foxes have holes, and birds of the air have nests; but the Son of Man has nowhere to lay his head" (v. 20). Another budding disciple makes a simple request, "Lord, first let me go and bury my father." Jesus' reply seems inflexible: "Follow me, and let the dead bury their own dead" (v. 22). Jesus tells us to let those who are numb and unresponsive to the kingdom of God put their own affairs to rest. In the very next scene, the disciples are following Jesus into a boat in order to cross the Sea of Galilee. Jesus is asleep when a storm threatens to flood the boat, and the disciples cry out, "Lord, save us!" (v. 25). Aboard the vessel with Jesus, they are a long way from the security of home.

It is interesting that the Gospel of Matthew does not begin with this theme of homelessness in relation to Jesus. On the contrary, it is unmistakably concerned with telling us where Jesus is from. Before telling us that Mary "was found to be with child from the Holy Spirit" (1:18), Matthew recounts "the genealogy of Jesus the Messiah, the son of David, the son of Abraham" (1:1). As son of Abraham, Jesus is the fulfillment of the promise. Recall the promise to Abraham in Genesis 12:2–3: "I will make of you a great nation, and I will bless you, and make your name great, so that you will be a blessing." As the son of David, Jesus is born into a royal lineage. He is the anointed one who, in the final days of his life, will enter Jerusalem with shouts of honor and admiration.

> Hosanna to the Son of David!
> Blessed is the one who comes in the name of the Lord!
> Hosanna in the highest heaven!
>
> Matthew 21:9

It is clear where Jesus belongs; his birthright and destiny is the throne.

The genealogy in Matthew makes Jesus' future evident through the storyline of its three parts—from promise to desolation to fulfillment. In the first part, fourteen generations are recounted between Abraham and David's kingship. Then, fourteen generations of Israel's kings are listed between David and the conquest of Jerusalem by the Babylonians (587 B.C.). At the conquest, the temple in Jerusalem is destroyed, and Judah's royalty and leading citizens are exiled to Babylon. This section of the list ends in desperate times. Finally, however, fourteen generations are registered between the Babylonian exile and Jesus' birth. The genealogy begins with the promise that is given to Abraham's descendants and ends with Jesus as that promise.

The genealogy in Matthew also tells us about the less-than-regal character of Jesus' lineage. The Son of God does not enter the clean and neat places of human history. By its ordinary and sometimes unseemly character, Jesus' human lineage witnesses to the hospitality of God. God does not enter an exceptional and unblemished line of human inheritance. For example, an angel must appear to Joseph in order to tell him that Mary's pregnancy is not reason for him to break their betrothal because "the child conceived in her is from the Holy Spirit." The angel addresses him as "Joseph, son of David" (1:20). In this way, Jesus' place among the Jewish people is emphasized through the genealogy's repetition of paternity ("Abraham was the father of Isaac, and Isaac was the father of Jacob, and Jacob was the father of Judah" and so on). Joseph's fatherhood is irregular and incredible, but the unusual nature of Jesus' birth does not separate Jesus from his people. On the contrary, Mary's conception of a child out of wedlock, Joseph's plan to quietly "dismiss" her (v. 19), and the appearance of the angel correspond to the messy and awkward succession of generations from Abraham to Joseph.

Note the following examples from Jesus' lineage: when the Lord appears to Abraham and Sarah to announce the promise of a son, Sarah cannot help but laugh; they are far too old to produce a child (Gen. 18:12). Nonetheless, Isaac is born in God's good time. The line from Abraham to Isaac then goes through Jacob, but by custom it should not. Jacob takes his place by swindling the birthright from his older twin Esau. Jacob also deceives his father, with the encouragement and help of his mother, so that he can become the recipient, in Esau's place, of his father's blessing of the firstborn.

From Abraham to David, two important women are mentioned. Matthew interrupts the pattern, "X was the father of Y," in order to stress that Tamar is the mother of Perez and that the line from Boaz to Jesse goes through Ruth. Tamar's husband died before they had children. When she seeks to take her rightful place in the household of Judah, she is denied. In response, she veils herself and presents herself to him as a prostitute. When she is found to be pregnant, Judah is enraged, until she reveals that he is the father (Gen. 38:12–30). She then takes her place. The next woman in the genealogy is well-known: Ruth is a Moabite married to a Judean. When she is widowed, she accompanies her mother-in-law, Naomi, to Naomi's homeland of Bethlehem. There Ruth serves Naomi by pressing her cause upon Boaz, marrying him, and bearing a son. This son of a Moabite is the grandfather of David.

Jesus, son of David, is the heir of the elderly and barren, con artists, and outsiders. But that is not all. Solomon, son of David and Bathsheba, is conceived through an unseemly course of events. Matthew stresses the point by noting that "David was the father of Solomon by the wife of Uriah" (1:6). David, remember, commits adultery, attempts to conceal the sin, and then arranges to have Uriah killed in battle. Afterward, Bathsheba enters David's household and Solomon is born. From Solomon to the Babylonian exile, not all in the succession of kings in the genealogy ennobles the line. Rehoboam refuses to listen to the people (1 Kings 12:15); he increases the burdens upon them, and he is unable to keep the northern tribes of Israel from dividing from Judah. Ahaz "made offerings on the high places, on the hills, and under every tree" (2 Kings 16:4), and he attempts to secure his reign by turning to the Assyrians rather than to God. In short, "he did not do what was right in the sight of the Lord his God, as his ancestor David had done, but he walked in the way of the kings of Israel" (2 Kings 16:2–3). Along with opportunists and foreigners like Jacob and Ruth, this part of the genealogy adds unfaithful kings, their mismanagement, and the steady downfall of their reign.

The end of the genealogy is unremarkable. It ends with a list of names, from Abuid to Matthan, that are not seen elsewhere in the Bible. This conclusion of the list also reveals where Jesus is from, the insignificant and unknown places. He is born in Bethlehem of Judea and as an infant takes flight to Egypt. He returns and is raised as a Nazarene. When he begins his ministry, he travels, teaches, and gathers disciples throughout Galilee, and despite his reputation in the region, he is not welcomed in his own hometown (Matt. 13:54–58; Luke 4:23–30). Toward the end of his life, he finds his way south to Jerusalem and is executed by crucifixion. By the standards of the Roman Empire, Jesus' birth and death deserve little notice.

"Foxes have holes, and birds of the air have nests; but the Son of Man has nowhere to lay his head." Jesus' homelessness can be deceptive. This human being is itinerant because he is God with us. Jesus Christ is God coming home to us, taking his place among us, and joining with us in our sometimes ignoble inheritance. He reaches out, touches the leper, and makes him whole (Matt. 8:1–4). When Jesus cleanses the leper in Matthew 8, he instructs the happy man to "say nothing to anyone," but to go and to show himself "to the priest, and offer the gift that Moses commanded, as a testimony to them" (v. 4). Jesus commands the man to say nothing, but the man is not told to keep the healing secret. This is hardly the case. Rather than spend time talking, he is told to go to the center of Jewish life, to the center point of their relation to God and to their gathering point as a people. There, in the center of things, the former leper will give testimony through an act of proper Jewish worship. The exiled leper will be welcomed home.

"Foxes have holes," but Jesus enters our homes, and by inviting him in, we might find ourselves a long way from the usual security of home. In Luke 19:1–10, Jesus was passing through Jericho and noticed a diminutive man watching him from the branches of a sycamore tree. He called out to the man, a tax collector, who was not only small in stature but also lacking in reputation. "Zacchaeus, hurry and come down; for I must stay at your house today" (v. 5). Zacchaeus was happy to do as he was told, but "all who saw it began to grumble and said, 'He has gone to be the guest of one who is a sinner'" (v. 7). While entertaining Jesus, however, Zacchaeus and his way of doing business were changed. "Look, half of my possessions, Lord, I will give to the poor; and if I have defrauded anyone of anything, I will pay back four times as much" (v. 8). Jesus has transformed Zacchaeus's home. Zacchaeus has been chosen to receive and give hospitality to Jesus, but Jesus has made his home less insular, less independent and self-sufficient, and less secure. Through hospitality to Jesus, Zacchaeus is restored to his own lineage as a son of Abraham and heir to God's blessing and promise. "Today salvation has come to this house, because he too is a son of Abraham. For the Son of Man came to seek out and to save the lost" (Luke 19:10).

When we confess that Jesus is the Lord and the only Son of God, we proclaim the reign of a homeless king. It is common in our day to think about royalty in fairytale places, in splendid castles with many rooms and servants. But our homeless king is the servant of all. We like to think about the carefree life of princes and princesses, but our Lord's pedigree is heavy with the burdens of human suffering and sin. The Son of God is sent to us, and his lordship is not set apart, not protected by high walls and soldiers. Our Lord takes his seat with us in our homes, and by opening our homes to him, we find reconciliation and peace. In this way of peace, we are called to proclaim his kingdom now in the everyday details of our lives among the people and in the places where we make our home. When we pray for the coming kingdom, we are able to do so because God is with us. Christ's Spirit is given to us as the Lord and giver of life.

24

The Holy Spirit, the Lord, the Giver of Life

■ At the inauguration of his ministry, Jesus was baptized by John. In Matthew's Gospel, the Spirit of God descended upon Jesus, and "a voice from heaven said, 'This is my Son, the Beloved, with whom I am well pleased'" (3:17). John was reluctant to baptize Jesus, because John had said that Jesus was far greater and would baptize the people "with the Holy Spirit and fire" (3:11). Nonetheless, it is fitting that Jesus first receives baptism from John, insofar as he also receives, rather than simply offers, the Spirit that is the love that flows in and from God. Writing at the beginning of the fifth century, Augustine calls the Holy Spirit the gift of God's very self. As "we say 'the gift of the giver' and 'the giver of the gift' . . . so the Holy Spirit is a kind of inexpressible communion or fellowship of Father and Son." Likewise, "it is God the Holy Spirit proceeding from God who fires man to the love of God and neighbor." In other words, it is through the gift of the Holy Spirit that we are able to love. The Spirit is the Lord and giver of life.

The Spirit gives life in unexpected ways and points us in unlikely directions. We ought not to forget that after the Spirit descends upon Jesus, he "was led up by the Spirit into the wilderness to be tempted by the devil" (Matt. 4:1). If the Spirit is the love that binds Father and Son—if the Spirit is the love that makes us adopted sons and daughters of God—what kind of love is this? What kind of love leads Jesus to a barren landscape? What kind of love leads him face to face with incredible enticements of power and possession? The devil tempts him to make stones into bread, to marshal God's angels for his own protection, and to worship the devil (and worship what is opposed to God) so that the kingdoms of the world will be at his feet.

The Gospel of Luke emphasizes similar themes. In Luke 3, John the Baptist is going into "all the region around the Jordan, proclaiming a baptism of repentance for the forgiveness of sins" (v. 3). His message is plain and severe. The time is at hand; the axe lies at the roots ready to cut down the barren trees, so bear good fruit. "What can we do?" the people ask. John gives practical instructions—nothing extraordinary or beyond our reach (vv. 10–14). "Whoever has two coats must share with anyone who has none; and whoever has food must do likewise." To tax collectors, "collect no more than the amount prescribed for you," and to soldiers, stop extorting money through threats and intimidation; "be satisfied with your wages." It all sounds easy; it sounds as though there must be more than this to preparing the way of the Lord.

The burden is easy, but John's call to share our coats and to ease our burdens may be more difficult because it is within our reach, too challenging because it is too close to home. By right of purchase and custom, most of us have and need several coats: a rain coat and a few cool weather jackets, a winter coat, an overcoat, and a few others hanging around. As a matter of doing their service to Rome, ancient tax collectors could collect too much and, as a consequence, overburden their clients. This right to make a considerable profit made the system work. Likewise, soldiers could intimidate a conquered people with impunity, press one person or another into service, and extort a good wage. Each act of coercion would help to show and intensify the rule of the empire. John's simple instructions to us, to tax collectors, and to soldiers demand risk and a radically new way of life.

After his baptism, Jesus brings the way of the Spirit too close to home. First, he is "filled with the Holy Spirit" and led into the wilderness and tempted (Luke 4:1–13). Then, in Luke 4:14, he is "filled with the power of the Spirit" upon his return to Galilee, and on the Sabbath day he enters the synagogue in his hometown of Nazareth. Standing before the congregation, he reads from the prophet Isaiah.

> The Spirit of the Lord is upon me,
> because he has anointed me to bring good news to the poor.
> He has sent me to proclaim release to the captives
> and recovery of sight to the blind,
> to let the oppressed go free,
> to proclaim the year of the Lord's favor.

Luke 4:18–19

What Spirit is this? And what would it mean to live by the life-giving Spirit of Christ?

"Today," Jesus tells those gathered in the synagogue, "this scripture has been fulfilled in your hearing." The people are amazed, but soon they begin to ask, "Is this not Joseph's son?" (4:21–22). They begin to be skeptical. Jesus responds by suggesting that foreigners will receive him more readily than these people of his own hometown. God's Spirit of hospitality will reach far beyond the chosen people of God. Jesus reminds them of Elijah who, in the time of great famine in Israel, was sent to the widow of Sidon instead. He also reminds them of Elisha who, despite the many lepers in Israel, healed only Naaman the Syrian. "When they heard this, all in the synagogue were filled with rage. They got up, drove him out of the town, and led him to the brow of the hill on which their town was built" (Luke 4:28–29). Jesus is homeless again (never to return to Nazareth). The people intended to throw him off the hill, and in doing so, they would enact just the kind of scene that the tempter in the wilderness had imagined. "On their hands they will bear you up, so that you will not dash your foot against a stone" (4:11). The angels, however, are not commanded to catch Jesus. Rather, he quietly passes through and goes on his way.

The Spirit leads us into a wilderness of temptations where there are plenty of opportunities to pledge our allegiance and to bow to things and people of the world. Yet, the coming of Jesus Christ, in the power of the Holy Spirit, is good news to the poor, liberty to the captives, and sight to the blind. An extra coat given to the poor, food to the hungry, and a new way of going about our business is the Spirit upon us. In Luke 4, the Spirit is upon Jesus, but there are no glorious angels. When the Spirit is upon us, there may be no legions from heaven, but there will be a lot of angry people. No stones are made into bread, but Jesus does have supper in Zacchaeus's house.

Receiving the Spirit and following in the way of discipleship means calling out to the tax collector (who is low in stature) and accepting hospitality in his home. When Jesus sends out his disciples "to proclaim the kingdom of God and to heal," he gives them "power and authority over all demons and to cure diseases" (Luke 9:1–2). In Matthew 10:2–4, the names of the twelve apostles are listed briefly, but the simple list reveals a lot. God's generosity is evident in Jesus' gathering and commissioning of the twelve. Among them are Peter and his brother Andrew, and James and his brother John, who all are fishermen called from their boats (Matt. 4:18–22). Also listed are Matthew, a tax collector, and Simon, a member of a Jewish faction who hoped and planned for rebellion against Roman rule (Luke 6:15). The list ends with Judas Iscariot, who betrays Jesus in Jerusalem. We should remember that Peter initially rejects Jesus' way to the cross (Matt. 16:21–23) and renounces Jesus in Jerusalem as well (Matt.

26:69–75). Brothers James and John, in what seems to be an immodest misunderstanding of the kingdom of God, ask to rule with Jesus, on his left hand and right (Mark 10:35–40). These are the Christ's representatives who will proclaim that the kingdom is drawing near.

When this contrary group is sent out to spread the good news, it is evident that their own transformation through the Spirit is also at stake. The tax collector is sent without a wallet, and the revolutionary without a staff or club. The fishermen have no food to offer, and the lieutenants on Jesus' left hand and right must suffer the rejection of hostile villages and towns. They will proclaim the nearness of the kingdom of heaven, and their entry into each place will be a sign that the kingdom is at hand:

> You received without payment; give without payment. Take no gold, or silver, or copper in your belts, no bag for your journey, or two tunics, or sandals, or a staff; for labors deserve their food. Whatever town or village you enter, find out who in it is worthy, and stay there until you leave.
>
> Matt. 10:8–11

If the apostles lack money and sandals, do they bring a sign of scarcity? Is the dawning of the kingdom marked by austerity measures? On the contrary, the twelve are not stripped of all provisions for their journey. They are clothed in the garments of peace, and they carry what is needed to be open to hospitality. They are armed with the good news and with the power to make people whole. They enter towns with the clothes, supplies, and instruments of expectation—anticipating a kingdom of bounty and peace.

Likewise, the Spirit that gives life and leads Jesus into the desert does not lead us to a rejection of the world. We are not sent out lacking the necessities of life. The Spirit brings bounty; it is the gift through which we are drawn into the love that unites the Father and the Son. The Spirit gathers and sends us out, only to be transformed and gathered again. In villages and towns, we are called to carry the possessions of peace and to be clothed in confidence that we will be received in peace. In the process, we become signs of the kingdom drawing near, sent out into the world "like sheep into the midst of wolves . . . [but] wise as serpents and innocent as doves" (Matt. 10:16).

25

One Holy Catholic and Apostolic Church

■ Being gathered by God's Spirit into the church means a particular way of being at home. We are like the disciples in Matthew 10 who are sent out to proclaim the good news. They are like Jesus, who invited himself into Zacchaeus's home. Like them, we are gathered and sent out, then gathered again. Being gathered into one holy catholic and apostolic church, we are on a journey home, anticipating hospitality and offering gifts of friendship and healing to our hosts. We are called to confidence in the way of Jesus Christ, to shed the possessions of self-reliance and to live by depending upon grace. Taking possession of peace, we are called to inhabit each city and household with hope. Being gathered into one holy church requires a certain kind of detachment and leaving home; yet the end in view is to share Christ's attachment and love for the world.

There is a Buddhist parable that is helpful in highlighting the fact that our everyday attachments bring great suffering and vulnerability. It is the story of the Buddha and a noblewoman, in whose mansion he lived for a time. One day she interrupts the Buddha; she is disheveled and distraught. She is seeking comfort and compassion because her granddaughter has died. The Buddha gives her consolation by asking her to imagine having a great number of grandchildren, as many as lived in the nearby city. The woman responds with encouragement; she would take immense joy in such a blessing. The Buddha suggests the contrary. She would never stop weeping. The death of her beloved granddaughter is not a unique experience. Countless people, including children and grandchildren, die in the city each day. Buddha's word of compassion gives a view of life that frees the noblewoman from her suffering. "They that hold a hundred dear, have a hundred sorrows. . . . They that hold nothing dear, have no sorrow. Free from grief are they—free from passion, free from despair. [W]hoever desires to be free from grief, free from passion, should hold absolutely nothing in this world dear."

As a philosophy of the East, this Buddhist release from attachments and suffering is not likely to resonate with us. For us, love and friendship are made evident in sharing each other's burdens. Although Buddhist detachment is unfamiliar, Christians have been attracted, from time to time, to a philosophy of the Greco-Roman world that encourages a more familiar form of detachment. In English, we sustain a bit of this view of life with use of the word "stoic," which comes from the Greek philosophy of Stoicism and, for us, means calmness and composure in the face of exciting pleasures and distressing pains. High-minded Greeks and Romans looked to become free from uncontrollable emotions and desires. They wanted to be free from uncontrollable circumstances of life. To be free, they endeavored to become virtuous, governed by reason, self-sufficient, and autonomous. By doing so, they could do what is good for others. They would, in fact, be good, and such goodness, unlike the pleasures of wealth and fame, cannot be taken away.

The Stoics aspired to be free from vulnerability to the ups and downs of life, accidents of chance, and the changing winds of fortune and misfortune. Freedom and self-sufficiency, they believed, could be found through acceptance of "things as they are" and through inner detachment from all that might bring suffering or change. This philosophy is attractive because it distinguishes the changeless good from various good things in life. It distinguishes our true good from fleeting pleasures. The highest goods of virtue and self-sufficiency are distinguished from limited goods, which are mere instruments for sustaining a good life.

Stoic philosophy has been attractive to Christianity because its conception of good is universal and based in the order of things, and because of its emphasis upon moral virtues. Because universal, the stoic way of life is available to everyone, landowner and laborer, rich and poor, strong and frail. I can stay where I am, accept the roles and duties before me, and be detached from the material possessions and social circumstances that are part of my place in life. This philosophy of life encourages social stability and self-assurance in one's own place. It cultivates inner balance and strength. It is attractive because it calls us to cultivate inner goodness in a world of impermanent and transitory goods.

Stoicism is the inverse of a modern form of hedonism. We in America have profound trust that we can find security and the good life through things, by good planning, and through just reparation for our suffering. We are a people who sue tobacco companies for our own smoking, and fast food restaurants for our weight. If we suffer misfortune, we assume someone will pay. Unlike the Stoics, we tend to think of happiness as a birthright. When neighborhoods are ruined by a hurricane, we have insurance to help us rebuild and hopefully make our homes better than before. If that hurricane were to cause deaths, we will blame the weather service for not giving us advanced warning, or for not predicting the storm's strength. We might blame home-builders or municipal codes for housing construction. Tobacco companies, fast food chains, weather forecasters, and contractors might be negligent and in the wrong. Their misdeeds are not the point. The point is that we are able to claim invulnerability to misfortune through technological and economic means. The good life and freedom are attained by building a fortress of things, rather than stoic acceptance, resolve, and detachment.

Like Stoicism, the Christian faith distinguishes God, as the highest good, from limited goods of wealth and honor, but, in contrast, our relationship to God (the highest good) opens us to a greater vulnerability. We are called to a life that highlights our lack of self-sufficiency. The God who takes on human flesh shows a particular way of greater attachment to the world (but a way of attachment that does not make a fortress of things). Christ is homeless because he is coming to stay with us. We are already far too detached (secured as we are in our own homes) in comparison to Christ's passion and way to the cross, in comparison to his touch upon the leper, and in comparison to his hospitality to outsiders and scoundrels. We are called to see Christ in those who are hungry and thirsty, those who are far from their homeland, those who need a shirt and shoes, those who are sick, and those confined to a prison cell (Matt. 25:31–46). These are the "places" where God is known, and to draw near to God, we will follow.

We are called to see and to participate in the universal good that is found in and with (not apart from) the changing world. God is with us, in Jesus Christ. Remember, this profession of faith is foolishness to the Greeks. In Jesus, the Stoics would not be able to imagine seeing God. "By the power of the Holy Spirit he was born of the Virgin Mary, and became human. For our sake he was crucified under Pontius Pilate; he suffered, died, and was buried." God is with us as a babe in a young woman's arms. He is a Jew, accused and executed under Roman rule. The one holy church is made in the image of this vulnerable body.

Today we remember the life and death of Jesus, and we mark our lives on Christmas and Easter with incongruent images: a poor babe in a manger, piles of toys brought by a jolly man, a great teacher and healer nailed to a cross, and the Easter bunny. Everyone from Charlie Brown to the teenager next door knows that the commercialization of Christmas (and Easter) is a problem. This year, in our town, one could witness a large plastic Santa Claus kneeling, with cattle and shepherds, before the baby Jesus. Our holy days are certainly distorted and misunderstood. However, the incongruity of our rituals and symbols offers a profound truth. The Son of God is dispossessed of his "place" in equality with God (Phil. 2:6–8), and he is born among us, a helpless and homeless babe. Jesus' death is the beginning of our new life. God's dispossession is our bounty.

What is this bounty? In God's dispossession, what do we come to possess? Francis of Assisi was deeply devoted to the babe in the manger. Among middle-class Americans, Francis has become the patron of birds, squirrels, and geraniums as he watches over our gardens with open arms. Francis, however, was the son of a well-to-do merchant, but he rejected his life of wealth and opportunity. He lived a life of poverty, not for the sake of freedom and not to be free from the sufferings of life, but to follow Jesus. "A disciple is not above the teacher, nor a slave above the master" (Matt. 10:24). I think that the babe in the manger is a popular image because we can imagine ourselves caring for Jesus, taking him into our homes, protecting him, and sharing our bounty with him. Francis recognized that "God with us" is our bounty and that we will find joy if we dare to follow and to find his place in the world.

The one holy catholic church is the body of Christ. Enter any church and you will find ordinary people who are gathered in God's name. The church is the rich and poor, sick and disabled, able and energetic, young and old, Peruvian and American, Philippino and Nigerian. This gathered body is not clothed as a merchant's son. This gathering is not like a televised awards show; too many toothless folk and bad haircuts are allowed in. This gathering is no United Nations, ready to offer new resolutions for ordering borders and sending troops throughout the world. It is no Rotary Club or the Junior League. The church is far more expansive and bountiful. We share in each other's suffering. Our wealth is the way of peace, and it is surprising how often we are willing to trade our riches in order to follow a way of self-possession and violence. The one universal church is a communion founded on the recognition and forgiveness of sins. The gathered people, who recognize sin and live by hope and peace, are a sign of God's place with us. Repentance is the first step in our understanding of Christ's love and attachment to the world; forgiveness is the foundation of the church.

26

The Forgiveness of Sin

■ After "We believe in one holy catholic and apostolic Church," we profess in the Nicene Creed that "We acknowledge one baptism for the forgiveness of sins." Baptism marks us as sons and daughters of God. It is the mark of our beginning and our destiny; we are made for union with God and our fellow human beings. This mark of our beginning and our end in God is the forgiveness of sins. When John the Baptist announces the coming of God's kingdom, he offers baptism for the forgiveness of sins. Likewise, when the Spirit descends upon the assembly on the day of Pentecost (Acts 2), Peter calls for repentance and offers baptism in the name of Jesus Christ for the forgiveness of sins. God raised Christ up; the power of death could not hold him. "[T]he promise is for you," Peter tells the people, "for your children, and for all who are far away, everyone whom the Lord our God calls to him" (Acts 2:39). We remember this day as the beginning of the church.

Like God's activity of creation, it is a mistake to think about forgiveness as something that is said in an instant and done. Recall a point made in chapters 21 and 22 that God's act of creation "out of nothing" is continuous with the ever-present activity of God in relation to us. Creation establishes nothing in God (as God is complete); rather, in being created by God we are continually given life in and through God. The same holds true for forgiveness.

Forgiveness of sin is the foundation of the new creation. We are made by God with the ability to know and to freely love the world and ourselves. Likewise, we can self-consciously respond to God, and freely desire and freely choose to respond in love. We sin when we freely and knowingly turn away. We are born into a world of sin, an inheritance of strife and the division of peoples (which makes baptism such a striking gesture about who we are). Forgiveness is God's response to the sin of the world through ongoing love. Forgiveness is what binds us to God and to each other. Forgiveness, rather than our goodness and holiness, is the foundation of the one holy church.

For years I have understood forgiveness through the image of a judge pounding a gavel and pronouncing that I am forgiven. This image, I think, is profoundly misleading. The judge comes to mind, I suspect, because of the parable of the unforgiving servant in Matthew 18:23–35. Jesus tells the story of a slave who pleads for more time to pay off his debt. The king does not give him an extension, but to the slave's amazement, the lord releases him from the debt. With a word from the king, it is done. But is it done? In understanding forgiveness in this way, I have made the very mistake that the slave makes in the parable. The forgiven servant thinks that it is done, so that when he encounters another slave who owes him money, he takes hold of the man's throat, demands payment, and has him thrown into prison. When the king hears of his action, the forgiven servant is delivered over "to be tortured until he would pay his entire debt" (v. 34). The unforgiving servant gets what he imagines his king to be, a judge who demands payment of a debt.

The unforgiving servant fails to understand forgiveness as a new way of living—a new way of being bound together with others, a new way of giving and receiving through the gift of grace, a new way of thinking about who we are called to be. Likewise, I had failed to understand forgiveness as God's ongoing response to the violence and anger of the world, and as a new way of responding to the world in imitation of God. In Matthew 18, the parable of the unforgiving servant follows Jesus' teaching about the process of forgiveness in the church (vv. 15–20) and Peter's question about how often one person should forgive another. "As many as seven times?" Jesus' response, "seventy times seven," suggests that the process will not end. This notion of a continuous activity points to the unforgiving servant's mistake. Forgiveness is not something we receive and then leave behind. Now my mistake: receiving God's forgiveness is not analogous to standing before a judge, but to a new way of standing before God and with our neighbors. Forgiveness is less like a judge's gavel and more like an epoxy or glue—a binding agent—for binding on earth what is bound in heaven (v. 18).

In order to highlight the binding nature of forgiveness, I would like to consider the example of domestic violence. In some respects, intimate partner violence is an extraordinary example, and it might be unwise to think about forgiveness, as an ordinary process, by means of this extraordinary case. On the other hand, domestic violence is not unusual. The U.S. Bureau of Justice reports that in 1999 over 670,000 women reported that they suffered assault or rape at the hands of their husband or boyfriend. Abuse is common in "loving" relationships, and sometimes harm is inflicted in the name of love and for the purposes of protecting the loving relationship. So, although it is an extreme example, domestic violence, if treated carefully, may give us insight on the ordinary course of forgiveness and what is required of us to forgive one another "seventy times seven."

Along with intimidation and abuse, part of the pathology of domestic violence is that the person who is beaten, whether an adult or child, blames herself or himself. In the common case of a woman who is attacked by her husband, she will be convinced by his rage and controlling behavior that she has done something wrong. He strikes out against her, but she will be concerned to say that she is sorry. She will try to change her behavior and the behavior of her children in order to appease him and to keep his anger at bay. Usually, their relationship is good (or seems good enough). The couple is able to keep up appearances by keeping his violence and abuse private. No one needs to know. He is a kind and caring husband and father, and he will express regret for the course of events. However, he will not accept responsibility or guilt. He regrets that he was *made* to strike out. He is sorry that it all happened, and he will promise never to hurt her again. He may even say (or demand), "Forgive me." But in doing so in private, he simply confirms the cycle of blame and abuse. How many times does an abuser say "never again"? He is like the unforgiving servant who accepts the clean slate of forgiveness ("it is done") and carries on as before.

For forgiveness to be complete, intervention into the structure of their relationship is required. She can truly forgive him, but for him to accept forgiveness, a change in their lives is required. Like affection or devotion from afar, a person can forgive someone who is unrepentant. I can love someone who does not return my love, but we should not call this love complete or whole or "true to itself" until the love is mutual and friendship is formed. Likewise, forgiveness without the other person's acceptance of guilt is possible, but it is forgiveness cut short and incomplete. In forgiveness, our habits of living together are at stake.

Matthew 18:15–20 outlines the process of forgiveness. The abused woman confronts her husband, and if he does not listen to her, she confronts him again with the help of a few friends. If this meeting fails, the man must deal with the whole church. If he continues to resist the truth about himself, "let such a one be to you as a Gentile and a tax collector" (v. 17). Is this "casting out" too harsh? Indeed, it is not. "Casting out" is a means of grace—if the "Gentile" refers to the centurion that Jesus encounters in Capernaum (Matt. 8:5), or if the "tax collector" means the likes of Zacchaeus (Luke 19:2), Matthew (Matt. 10:3), or the one filled with shame and praying in the temple with the Pharisee (Luke 18:13). Biblically speaking, the "Gentiles" are outsiders and idolaters, and the tax collectors are those whose way of doing business sets them over against their community. They are not without hope. The centurion is able to show uncharacteristic faith, and Zacchaeus is able to turn his life around. Likewise, if the abusive man refuses to take responsibility and to accept forgiveness and to live a new way, the woman cannot continue to live with him. He should be treated as a person who has set himself apart, who needs the hospitality and grace of Christ. Remember the message of John the Baptist: repent and make the way straight; change the way you go about your business.

Forgiveness in less extraordinary circumstances has the same structure and operation. We say or hear "I am sorry," and the customary response is "that's OK." I try not to be defensive and critical, even though I am hurt by another's actions. When I hear "sorry," I seem to be able to put my grievances aside for a moment. I want to be mature and affirming, confident and self-possessed. I say, "That's OK," which means "Don't worry about me—I'll be OK; I can handle it, I'm fine." My response is appropriate on some occasions, when wronged by an acquaintance or stranger, for example. Perhaps we crash our shopping carts or knock bumpers in the parking lot. There's no damage; it's fine. The response is fitting, so that we can politely go on our way. But "Don't worry about it; it's OK" has become a habit even with my loved ones and friends. It has become my immediate response whenever someone says, "I'm sorry."

I cut the process short, and by doing so, I do not treat forgiveness as a different way of going about business. Like the unforgiving servant, I carry on with business as usual. Like the abusive husband, I use "forgiveness" and "I'm sorry" in a shallow way so that I do not have to face problems and make changes. I say, "It's OK," in a way that seems to mean that we really do not need forgiveness, that we can avoid the whole complicated process, that we can make it easy on ourselves. Rather than "It's OK," we ought to begin with, "Something is going wrong" or "I/We have a problem." In truth, the process of forgiveness is not affirming at the start, and it does not allow me to be secure and self-possessed. Because they require risk, everyday opportunities for repentance and forgiveness constitute a process of transformation. In the ordinary course of our lives, we can learn to be open to grace.

When "we acknowledge one baptism for the forgiveness of sins," we accept that God's grace will make us a new people. In baptism, we are given a new beginning, with the grace-given capacity to respond to God in faith and to live out the love of God that is ours through Jesus Christ. To believe in one holy catholic and apostolic \church is to hope that we will be created anew—not privately, but as a community, gathered as the body of Christ and as a sign of God's creative activity and attachment to the world.

27

Resurrection and the Life of the World to Come

■ "We look for the resurrection of the dead and the life of the world to come." This statement of faith concludes the Nicene Creed. It is the declaration of a destiny beyond our present existence and what might seem to be a contradictory affirmation of our bodily nature. The fit between our future with God and our unavoidably material existence is not easy to imagine. Very early in our history, the church struggled against the view that our bodies were only obstacles to the spirit, or obviously evil—prisons from which our true selves, our spirits, must be liberated. Our profession of faith in the resurrection of the dead states the contrary, that God created human beings, body and spirit, and "it was good." Our faith is that God's activity of our redemption—the sending of the Son—is the grace of a new creation. The new way of the life-giving Spirit is a transformation of bodies and our place in creation as well.

Paul makes this line of reasoning plain in Romans 8:22. "We know that the whole of creation has been groaning in labor pains until now; and not only the creation, but we ourselves, who have the first fruits of the Spirit, groan inwardly while we wait for adoption, the redemption of our bodies." In 1 Corinthians 15:12–58, he deals directly with the problem of the resurrection of the body. In this section of the letter, he answers questions and doubts among the Corinthians about the possibility of our bodies being

166

raised. It must be so, Paul is convinced. "If Christ is proclaimed as raised from the dead, how can some of you say there is no resurrection of the dead?" (v. 12). We might ask, "Will there be corpses walking about, like in *The Night of the Living Dead*?" To answer, Paul uses the analogy of a seed. What dies and is planted is not the same as what springs from the ground. "It is sown a physical body, it is raised a spiritual body" (v. 44). We have borne the image of human beings created from dust, and we will bear "the image of the man of heaven" (v. 49). Yes, Paul admits, it is a great mystery, but at the center of our faith is the redemption of the body—of creation and our relation to creation, people, places, and things.

Such a profession of faith has far-reaching implications for how we understand the relationship between our souls and bodies, our spiritual and material creation. They cannot be divided. We cannot do one thing with our bodies and claim the opposite for our spirit. One familiar example is the Christian rejection of casual sex. We cannot give our bodies to another and remain personally and spiritually detached. A less obvious example is the idea that where, how, and with whom we live every day become part of who we are.

If my wife and I were to win the lottery, our use of our millions would make a difference to who we are and who we are becoming. If we were to buy our dream house, we could live far from the problems of our neighbors, and near the school of our choice. Each of our children could have their own rooms, TVs, computers, cell phones, and new clothes. No more hand-me-downs. No more sports equipment from yard sales. No more thrift store blenders and crock pots. No more car worries. Perhaps, we would buy a fashionable SUV, and my children would no longer be embarrassed when I drop them off at school. I would not have to embarrass myself with my fifteen-year-old jackets and ties. We could correct the things about ourselves that have bothered us for a long time. We could even out imbalances and straighten crooked lines with cosmetic surgery.

With a few million dollars, our everyday lives would not be the same, and we would take a different "place" in the world. When all is said and done, I could not claim that I am simply the same person as before. Such a claim would divide body and spirit—a prideful separation from the very things and way of life that I want to make my own. I could not tell my old friends, "I am just the same guy you used to know." We would change less, I suppose, if we were to give our million dollars away. Such a radical act would bring clarity to our lives. We would have to make a bold decision about who we are and what we want, and with such a decisive act, it is hard to imagine that we would carry on thinking about our lives and living them the same as before. For good or ill, we are changed by our use of money and things.

How ought we to live? This is an old question. "Do not trust in your righteousness, do not worry about the past, but control your tongue and your stomach." Learn humility, receive grace, live for "the world to come," and do so by paying heed to your words and your body. This is the counsel of Antony, who set out into the Egyptian desert, at the end of the third century. Setting out into the wilderness in about 285, his plan was to live according to the Spirit and to prepare for life in the heavenly household of God.

Antony's journey is much different from our own (if you have a warm bed and full refrigerator like me). With wholehearted determination, he seeks to undertake the instructions of Matthew 6:25–33 as a consistent habit of life. "Do not worry about your life, what you will eat or what you will drink . . . . But strive first for the kingdom of God and his righteousness, and all these things will be given to you as well" (vv. 25, 33). Following this way, Antony endures a life of fasting and other severe disciplines. His self-imposed regimen is likely to appear to modern Christians to be a rejection of his body, but this is hardly the case. For Antony and the ascetics of his time, the body is united with the spirit. He knows that humility and dependence upon God begin with the stomach. In comparison, we are more inclined to divide body and spirit, to assume that our stomachs and appetites have nothing to do with the way we pray. Antony strives for poverty of spirit and spiritual restoration; to do so, he endeavors to be poor.

The story of Antony's journey into the desert begins when the words of Matthew 19:21 press upon him through what he understands to be providential events. While on his way to church, he ponders the lives of the apostles and the accounts in the Acts of the Apostles, where people "had sold their possessions and brought the proceeds to lay at the apostles' feet for distribution to those in need." Antony then enters the church precisely at the moment that Matthew 19:21 is read, "If you wish to be perfect, go, sell your possessions, and give the money to the poor, and you will have treasure in heaven; then come, follow me."

Upon hearing this command, Antony gives up the comforts of his home and sets out on a course of rigorous discipline and constant self-evaluation. He sells and gives away the proceeds of his considerable estate, and he trusts his sister to a community of religious women. Antony's voluntary poverty is as much spiritual as material; each is the medium of the other. The spiritual and physical are connected so deeply that in his temptations and spiritual struggles, Antony actually exchanges blows with demons. In the desert, he must face silver and gold that have been put in his path. The silver, he discovers, is a demonic illusion, but "it is not clear whether the devil put [the gold] there to deceive him or whether heavenly power revealed it to prove that Antony could not be seduced even by real riches."

Essential to Antony's struggles of the spirit is his unwillingness to accept glory that is due to God alone. Poverty means nothing to him if he does not learn spiritual dependence. His strength of spirit is evident in his healing power, but as the wonders increase, he is increasingly vigilant against the temptations of pride. Like Christ, he heals the daughter of a military officer without seeing or touching her. In Antony's case, however, he refuses even to see the military officer. Refusing to open the door to his cell, Antony sends the soldier and his daughter away, "I too am mortal and share your weakness. But if you believe in Christ whose servant I am, go and pray to God according to your faith and your daughter will be healed."

Antony's life is a parable for us. In the severity of his life, there is an excess that makes plain the relationship of body and spirit. When Antony succeeds in disciplining his body through fasting, keeping vigil night and day, and constant prayer, his spirit is strengthened. When his contest with the devil is virtually won, and as his spirit is strengthened through austerities, his body is all the more beautiful in its countenance and dignified in its bearing. Even in death, "his body looked healthier than those glistening bodies which are pampered by baths and luxurious living." His body is enlivened by his purity of heart. In his life, he performs Jesus' instruction: "strive first for the kingdom of God and his righteousness, and all these things will be given to you as well." In living these words, the promise is fulfilled. Antony's life is a parable of the restoration and renewal (the resurrection) of our bodies.

To those who follow him into the desert, Antony provides a rule for desert monasticism and instructions on the Christian life. He counsels monks not to be proud of their dispossession, and he suggests detachment for all. He points out that what is given up in this world is slight compared to what we will receive, for "the whole earth, compared to the infinity of the heavens, is small and limited." We ought to live for God, and to seek after what leads to eternal life:

> Let Christians care for nothing that they cannot take away with them. We ought rather to seek after that which will lead us to heaven, namely wisdom, chastity, justice, virtue, an ever watchful mind, care of the poor, firm faith in Christ, a mind that can control anger, hospitality. Striving after these things, we shall prepare ourselves a dwelling in the land of the peaceful.

"Blessed are the poor in spirit, for theirs is the kingdom of heaven. . . . Blessed are the meek, for they will inherit the earth. . . . Blessed are the peacemakers, for they will be called children of God" (Matt. 5: 3, 5, 9). For Antony, purity of heart begins when we live without fear and no longer cling to earthly possessions, both material and spiritual. For Antony, the journey begins with our words, our money, and our stomachs.

169

Conclusion

■ Certainly, Antony's journey into the desert is not the only way or the most obvious or prominent way for Christians. However, the intensity of his life reveals a truth for us all. Our faith, particularly our faith in the resurrection, requires that we attend to the habits of the body, our relation to things, and how our bodily habits and possessions set us in good company with (or against) God and neighbor. When we say "we believe," we are called to the disruptive friendship and hospitality of God. We are called to share and to be the body of Christ. We are called to repentance and forgiveness, and to take our place in the world by following Jesus. We are called to peace and to hope. We are called to cultivate the good of creation and to apply our ownership and mastery over things to the good of common life in God.

Antony's enterprise in the desert is a parable for our middle-class life in an imperial economy. His sojourn in the wilderness was a means for him and those like him (such as Mother Synclitica) to put the customs of the city at a distance and to learn new ways of life—new ways of encountering the neighbor and stranger, and seeing and depending upon God. Likewise, our faith is a venture of seeing the world as God's creation—to see the world (like baby Daniel) as a sea of grace. Our faith is a venture of sharing God's grace and peace, and by doing so, taking our place in a home where God in Christ is our guest.

A Final Word: Bound to Love

■ The love of God is unmerited, but it is not unconditional. In other words, love is free but incredibly challenging. These statements might seem like contradictions, but they point to the heart of the Christian's call to love. On one hand, God's grace is free and unearned, while, on the other hand, it brings repentance, forgiveness, judgment, and transformation. These two sides of God's love have been operating as themes throughout the book. The grace of God is surprising and inexhaustible, and to acknowledge the astounding presence of God's love in the world, we may need to see through the eyes of Zacchaeus or the tax collector in the temple, the baptized child or Antony of Egypt, a prison inmate or the laborer who works little and is paid much (Matt. 20:1–16). We will have to see the world in a strange new way that actually puts the ordinary matters of our lives—the people, places, and things—into better focus. Love is not unconditional because it is conditioned by the good of life. God's unmerited love is demanding, as it puts our eyes upon heaven so that we might be more deeply bound to the earth.

Love is free. This first point might seem more obvious than the idea that love has conditions and makes demands. The love of God is a gift; therefore, we do not earn reconciliation and community with God and our neighbors. This point appears understandable, but the grace of community is not easy to put into practice. In the usual course of things, we work and play among people with whom we share mutual benefit, interests, and talents. We stay near to friends who are like us in temperament and outlook. We build each other up. Because good friendships are a lifetime achievement, it is hard, sometimes, to remember that we receive God's friendship only through grace. We all are babes dipped into a sea of God's love for the world. It is easy to forget that we find ourselves gathered as the church simply because we have been called (not because we are good), and that we are called "to be ourselves" most boldly in worship.

Given the usual course of human friendships, the friendship of God is often experienced as disruptive. Friends share a history of life together and common purposes. Friends share mutual friends. The friendship of God is similar, but also very different. Indeed, God in Christ draws near to us in an offer of self-giving love, and we cannot in any sense claim that we merit this gracious mutuality and shared life with God. God's friendship is freely given. In this freedom, we are called to be friends of God's friends. Through Jesus Christ, we share in God's love, and divine life is now ours to live by. In receiving the gift of God, our lives become the very "condition" and "measure" of our love. The love of God in us is conditioned by—bound, formed, and directed to—the goodness of God.

Precisely because love is a gift, it must be conditioned by grace. It is conditioned by the self-giving love of God. God's love is conditioned by the self-emptying of Jesus Christ (Phil. 2), and by his life, words, death, and resurrection. In this regard, the popular view of "unconditional" love makes little sense. Unconditional love seems to mean that a person can experience and express love without care for who we are together or where we are going and how we will live. In this view, "love means never having to say you're sorry." This sense of unconditional love (as opposed to unmerited grace) separates our soulful experiences of love from our concrete actions. With this view of love, the spirit is separated from the body, and we Christians are often tempted by the ease of this separation. But we confess faith in God who creates heaven and earth. We confess that God is with us in the flesh and is raised in the flesh. We confess that the Holy Spirit is the Lord and giver of life. This book as a whole (dealing with people, places, things, God, and creation) follows along the way of our confession of faith. I have attempted to think through how our bodies and lives together are bound, formed, and directed to love. I have tried to imagine what we middle-class Americans will say when, like Zacchaeus, we entertain the Lord in our homes.

Bibliography

Chapter 1

Hansen, Kristin A. "Seasonality of Moves and Duration of Residence." Economic and Statistics Administration, U.S. Department of Commerce, October 1998.

Chapter 2

———."GE Power Systems Gains $2B Contract." *Daily Gazette* (March 14, 2000).

———. "Mayor Jurczyski's Big Chill." *Albany Times Union* (April 14, 1996).

———. "Schenectady Officials Lambaste GE Over New Round of Layoffs, Councilmen, Duci Accuse Firm of Misinforming City." *Albany Times Union* (February 28, 1995).

Bellah, Robert N., Richard Madsen, Wiliam M. Sullivan, Ann Swindler, and Steven M. Tipton. *Habits of the Heart: Individualism and Commitment in American Life.* Berkeley: University of California Press, 1985.

D'Errico, Richard A. "GE comes full circle." *The Business Review* (Albany), Jan. 28, 2002.

Mishel, Lawrence, Jared Bernstein, and John Schmitt. *The State of Working America 1998–99.* Ithaca: ILR Press/Cornell University, 1999.

Chapter 3

Hauerwas, Stanley, and Charles Pinches. *Christians Among the Virtues.* Notre Dame, Ind.: University of Notre Dame, 1997.

Lewis, C. S. "Friendship." In *The Four Loves.* New York: Harcourt Brace and Company, 1988.

Chapter 5

Derrett, J. Duncan. *Law in the New Testament.* London: Darton, Longman, and Todd, 1970.

Chapter 6

Augustine. *The Confessions.* Trans. Maria Boulding, O.S.B. Ed. John E. Rotelle, O.S.A. Hyde Park, N.Y.: New City Press, 1997.

Chapter 7

Augustine. *The Works of Saint Augustine: Marriage and Virginity.* Trans. Ray Kearney. Ed. David G. Hunter. Hyde Park, N.Y.: New City Press, 1999.

John Paul II, "Letter to Families." In Origins: CNS Documentary Service 23 (March 3, 1994) 37: 683–659.

Chapter 8

Lewis, C. S. "Eros." In *The Four Loves.* New York: Harcourt Brace and Company, 1988.

Thatcher, Adrian. *Living Together and Christian Ethics.* Cambridge: Cambridge University Press, 2002.

Chapter 10

Krakauer, Jon. *Into the Wild.* New York: Anchor Books, 1997.

Lennon, John. "All You Need is Love," http://www.thebeatlesongs.com/all_you_need_is_love.htm ; "Give Peace a Chance," http://www.sing365.com/music/lyric.nsf/SongUnid/9F2280B3491B5F3F48256BCA00089770 ; "Imagine," http://www.john-lennon.com/#words.

Chapter 12

Day, Dorothy. *By Little and By Little.* Ed. Robert Ellsberg. New York: Knopf, 1984.

Chapter 13

———. "America the Beautiful." In *The United Methodist Hymnal.* Nashville, Tenn.: The United Methodist Publishing House, 1989.

Hauerwas, Stanley. "September 11, 2001: A Sermon a Year Later." *Ekklesia Project Online,* http://www.ekklesiaproject.org/webzine.html.

Lewis, C. S. "Likings and Loves for the Sub-Human." In *The Four Loves.* New York: Harcourt Brace and Company, 1988.

National Conference of Catholic Bishops, "The Harvest of Justice is Sown in Peace" (November 17, 1993), http://www.nccbuscc.org/sdwp/harvest.htm.

Chapter 14 and the Conclusion of Part Two

King, Martin Luther Jr. *The Strength to Love.* Philadelphia: Fortress, 1981.

McKibben, Bill. *The End of Nature.* New York: Doubleday, 1999.

Chapter 15

Campbell, Colin. "Consuming Goods and the Good of Consuming." In *Consumer Society in American History.* Ed. Lawrence B. Glickman. Ithaca: Cornell University Press, 1999.

Csikszentmihalyi, Mihaly, and Eugene Rochberg-Halton. "The Most Cherished Objects in the Home." In *The Meaning of Things: Domestic Symbols and the Self.* Cambridge: Cambridge University Press, 1981.

Csikszentmihalyi, Mihaly. *Flow: The Psychology of Optimal Experience.* New York: Harper and Row, 1990.

Chapter 16

McGuinneas, Maya. "Plastic People," *Washington Monthly* 33:5 (May 2001).

Manning, Robert D. *Credit Card Nation: The Consequences of America's Addition of Credit.* New York: Basic Books, 2000.

Chapter 17

Avila, Charles. "Ambrose: Born Naked" and "John Chrysostom: You are Possessed by Possessions." In *Ownership: Early Christian Teaching.* Maryknoll, N.Y.: Orbis Books, 1983.

Schudson, Michael. "Delectable Materialism: Second Thoughts on Consumer Culture." In *Consumer Society in American History.* Ed. Lawrence B. Glickman. Ithaca: Cornell University Press, 1999.

Swan, Laura. *The Forgotten Desert Mothers: Sayings, Lives, and Stories of Early Christian Women.* New York: Paulist Press, 2001.

Chapter 18

Sayers, Dorothy L. *Creed or Chaos.* New York: Harcourt and Brace, 1949.

Chapter 21

Barron, Robert. *Thomas Aquinas: Spiritual Master.* New York: Crossroad Publishing Company, 1996.

McCabe, Herbert, O.P. "Creation" and "The Involvement of God." In *God Matters.* Springfield, Ill.: Templegate Publishers, 1991.

Crosby, Michael, ed. *Solanus Casey: The Official Account of a Virtuous American Life.* New York: Crossroad Publishing Company, 2000.

Portier, William L. *Tradition and Incarnation: Foundations of Christian Theology.* New York: Paulist Press, 1994.

Chapter 22

"Akkadian Myths and Epics." In *Ancient Near East Texts, Relating to the Old Testament,* ed. James B. Pritchard. 3rd ed., with Supplement. Princeton: Princeton University Press, 1969.

Lewis, C. S. "Charity." In *The Four Loves.* New York: Harcourt Brace and Company, 1988.

Chapter 23

McCabe, Herbert, O.P. "The Geneology of God." In *God Matters.* Springfield, Ill.: Templegate Publishers, 1991.

Chapter 24

Augustine. *The Trinity.* Trans. Edmund Hill, O.P. Brooklyn: New City Press, 1991.

Chapter 25

Burlingame, Eugene Watson, trans. *Buddhist Parables.* New Haven: Yale University Press, 1922.

Chapter 26

Miles, Al. *Domestic Violence: What Every Pastor Needs to Know.* Minneapolis: Fortress Press, 2000.

Rennison, Callie Marie. "Intimate Partner Violence and Age of Victim." U.S. Department of Justice: Bureau of Justice Statistics, 2001. http://www.ojp.usdoj.gov/bjs/pub/pdf/ipva99.pdf.

Chapter 27

"Life of Antony by Athanasius." In *Early Christian Lives,* trans. Carolinne White. London: Penguin, 1998.

McCarthy, David. "The Gospels Embodied." In *Cambridge Companion to the Gospels,* ed. Stephen Barton. Cambridge: Cambridge University Press, 2004.

Ward, Benedicta, S.L.G., trans. *The Sayings of the Desert Fathers.* London: A. R. Mowbray and Co. LTD, 1975.

A Final Word

Pieper, Josef. *Faith, Hope, Love.* San Francisco: Ignatius Press, 1997.

Zacchaeus as model & metaphor

friendship w/ God - &
Friends of God's friends

Ron P. & the $1000
- mixed messages re
wealth .

is it enough?